KT-463-293

access to sociology

RELIGION

Paul Selfe & Mark Starbuck

Series Editor: Paul Selfe

WORCESTER COLLEGE
OF TECHNOLOGY

0110764

Hodder & Stoughton

A MEMBER OF THE HODDER HEADLINE GROUP

Order queries: please contact Bookpoint Ltd, 130 Milton Park, Abingdon, Oxon OX14 4SB. Telephone: (44) 01235 827720, Fax: (44) 01235 400454. Lines are open from 9.00 – 6.00, Monday to Saturday, with a 24 hour message answering service.

A catalogue record for this title is available from The British Library

ISBN 0 340 711825

First published 1998
Impression number   10 9 8 7 6 5 4
Year   2003   2002

Copyright © 1998, Paul Selfe and Mark Starbuck

All rights reserved. This work is copyright. Permission is given for copies to be made of pages provided they are used exclusively within the institution for which this work has been purchased. For reproduction for any other purpose, permission must first be obtained in writing from the publishers.

Paul Selfe and Mark Starbuck have asserted the moral right to be identified as the authors of this work

Cover photo: M.C. Escher 'Bond of Union' © Cordon Art B.V - Baarn - Holland

Typeset by Transet Limited, Coventry, England.
Printed in Great Britain for Hodder & Stoughton Educational, a division of Hodder Headline plc, 338 Euston Road, London NW1 3BH by The Bath Press, Bath

CONTENTS

ACKNOWLEDGEMENTS

All authors are familiar with the pressures and demands of writing. It is therefore of great assistance to have a supportive friend and family network. For Mark Starbuck, the wonderful enthusiastic encouragement of his wife, Rebecca, and the thoughtful advice of Allan and Annette Voak was greatly appreciated. In the same way, thanks are due to Lorna, Jessica and Amy Selfe for their constant enjoyment and interest in the project. We are both most grateful to all the sociology students of Jersey College for Girls, who have tried and tested many of the activities in the book, and to colleagues who read and commented on chapters. We have have also received extremely thorough and constructive guidance from Anna Clark and Llinos Edwards and their colleagues in the organisation and production of this and other books in the series. It has been a great pleasure to work with them.

The publishers would like to thank James Hunkin for permission to reproduce his photographs in this book.

The book is dedicated especially to Rebecca and Graham.

1

INTRODUCTION

HOW TO USE THE BOOK

EACH CHAPTER IN this book examines one or more of the central debates relating to the sociology of religion. The text is devised for readers with little or no background knowledge in the subject, and there are Study Points and Activities throughout to encourage a consideration of the issues raised. Student readers are advised to make use of these and answer them either on paper or in group discussion, a particularly fruitful way of learning; they will assist them to develop the skills of interpretation, analysis and evaluation. There are many ways of preparing for an exam, but a thorough understanding of the material is obviously crucial.

Each chapter is structured to give a clear understanding of the authors, concepts and issues that you need to know about. To assist understanding and facilitate later revision, it is often helpful to make concise notes.

MAKING NOTES FROM THE BOOK

Linear notes
- Bold headings establish key points: names, theories and concepts.
- Subheadings indicate details of relevant issues.
- A few numbered points list related arguments.

Diagram or pattern notes
- Use a large blank sheet of paper and write a key idea in the centre.
- Make links between this and related issues.
- Show also the connections between sub issues which share features in common.

Both systems have their advantages and disadvantages, and may take some time to perfect. Linear notes can be little more than a copy of what is already in the book and patterned notes can be confusing. But if you practise the skill, they can reduce material efficiently and concisely becoming invaluable for revision. Diagrammatic notes may be very useful for those with a strong visual memory and provide a clear overview of a whole issue, showing patterns of interconnection. The introduction of helpful drawings or a touch of humour into the format is often a good way to facilitate the recall of names, research studies and complex concepts.

Activity
• Make a diagram to show the two ways of making notes with their possible advantages and disadvantages

SKILLS ADVICE

Students must develop and display certain skills for their examination and recognise which ones are being tested in a question. The clues are frequently in key words in the opening part. The skill domains are:

1 **Knowledge and understanding:** the ability to discuss the views of the main theorists; their similarities and differences; the strengths and weaknesses of evidence. To gain marks students must display this when asked to *explain, examine, suggest a method, outline reasons.*
2 **Interpretation, application and analysis:** the use of evidence in a logical, relevant way, either to show how it supports arguments or refutes them. Students must show this ability when asked *identify, use items A/B/C, draw conclusions from a table.*
3 **Evaluation:** the skill of assessing evidence in a balanced way so that logical conclusions follow. Students can recognise this skill when asked to *assess, critically examine, comment on levels of reliability, compare and contrast,* or if asked *to what extent.*

Activity
Draw an evaluation table, as below, using the whole of an A4 page. Examine studies as you proceed in your work and fill in the relevant details. Keep it for revision purposes.

Sociologist		
Title of the study	Strengths	Weaknesses
Verdict		
Judgement/justification		

REVISION ADVICE

- Keep clear notes at all times in a file or on disk (with back up copy).
- Be familiar with exam papers and their demands.
- Become familiar with key authors, their theories, their research and sociological concepts.

Activity

Make and keep **Key Concept Cards**, as shown below.

COLLECTIVE CONSCIENCE

Key idea

A term used by **Durkheim** meaning:

- The existence of a social and moral order exterior to individuals and acting upon them as an independent force.
- The shared sentiments, beliefs and values of individuals which make up the **collective conscience.**
- In **traditional societies** it forms the basis of social order.
- As societies modernise the collective conscience weakens: **mechanical solidarity** is replaced by **organic solidarity**.

Key theorist: Emile Durkheim

Syllabus area: Sociological Theories of Religion: Functionalism

EXAMINATION ADVICE

To develop an effective method of writing, answers should be:

- **Sociological:** use the language and research findings of sociologists; do not use anecdotal opinion gathered from people not involved in sociology to support arguments.

- **Adequate in length:** enough is written to obtain the marks available.
- **Interconnected** with other parts of the syllabus (such as stratification, gender, ethnicity).
- **Logical:** the answer follows from the relevant evidence.
- **Balanced:** arguments and counter arguments are weighed; references are suitable.
- **Accurate:** reliable data is obtained from many sources.

The three skill areas on p 2 should be demonstrated, so that the question is answered effectively.

In displaying knowledge, the student is not necessarily also demonstrating interpretation.

- This must be specified with phrases like 'Therefore, this study leads to the view that…'
- Sections of answers should hang together, one leading to the next. This shows how the question is being answered by a process of analysis based on the evidence.
- Reach a conclusion based on the evidence used and the interpretations made.

The skill of evaluation is often regarded (not necessarily accurately) as the most problematic. Evaluation means being judge and jury; the strengths and weaknesses of evidence is assessed and an overall judgement about its value is made. To evaluate an argument or theory, consider whether it usefully opens up debate; explains the events studied; does it have major weaknesses?

Activity
Look through some past examination papers and pick out the evaluation questions. Underline the evaluation words and work out which skills are required.

COURSEWORK ADVICE

Coursework provides an opportunity to carry out a study using primary and/or secondary data to investigate an issue of sociological interest, and must address theoretical issues. The suggestions included at the end of each chapter may be adapted or used to generate further ideas. Final decision must be agreed with a teacher or tutor.

MAKING A PLAN

Before starting a piece of coursework, you should make a plan:

1 Read and make notes from articles describing research projects in journals.
2 Have a clear aim in mind; choose an issue that interests you and is within your ability.
3 Decide more precisely what you want to know; establish a simple hypothesis to test.
4 Select a range of possible methods; consider both quantitative and qualitative.
5 Decide on a range of possible sources of information.
6 List the people to whom you can seek help, perhaps including a statistician.

WRITING THE PROJECT

1 Seek frequent advice from a teacher or tutor.
2 Check the weighting for different objectives in the marking scheme.
3 Keep clear notes throughout, including new ideas and any problems that arise.
4 Limit its length (maximum 5,000 words).
5 Label and index the study in the following way:
  a **Rationale:** a reason for choosing the subject; preliminary observations on the chosen area
  b **Context:** an outline of the theoretical and empirical context of the study
  c **Methodology:** a statement of the methodology used and reasons for selecting it
  d **Content:** presentation of the evidence and/or argument including results
  e **Evaluation:** the outcomes are weighed and strengths and weaknesses noted.
  f **Sources:** all the sources of information are listed.

2

THE SIGNIFICANCE OF RELIGION IN SOCIETY

Introduction

THIS CHAPTER LOOKS at the nature and interpretation of religion and the meaning of superstition and magic. Patterns of religious behaviour are studied by sociologists because they appear in every society in the world in some form or another, and therefore represent an ancient and highly influential social institution. The sociology of religion examines the role and the significance of religion in society; how beliefs and practices can affect behaviour; how religion is perceived and understood; its influences on social life and the factors which influence the way it is organized.

Table 1: *Theorists, concepts and issues in this chapter*		
KEY THEORISTS	KEY CONCEPTS	KEY ISSUES
Emile Durkheim	Sacred and profane Ritual	• The problems of defining religion
Max Weber	Rationality Meaning	• Significance of ritual, myth and doctrine
Peter Worsley	Magic Superstition	• The dimensions of religion
Milton Yinger	Functional equivalent	• The distinctions between magic, religion, superstition and magic
Ninian Smart	Religious dimensions Myth	
Peter Berger and Thomas Luckmann	A moral world Sacred canopy	

The sociology of religion is not directly concerned with philosophical or theological issues such as the existence of God, or the relative merits of different kinds of religious organisations and their belief systems.

WHAT IS RELIGION?

The definition of religion is not straightforward. It is a complex and varied phenomenon that is interpreted in many different ways.

Firstly, what constitutes religious behaviour? Does it include:

- acts of superstition or the belief in astrology?
- an aboriginal ritual in which people hold to their stomachs a slat of wood on the end of a cord (known as a bull-roarer), to obtain some mystical powers it possessed?
- football fans who wear lucky scarves, worship their key players, attend matches every week, sing the team's songs, and have their lives transformed by their attachment to the club?

Secondly, what are the qualities which define an organisation as a major religion? There is common agreement that Christianity, Judaism, Islam, Hinduism and Buddhism are religions even though they show major variations in their practices. They do not all have a single supreme deity at the centre; one is polytheistic, while another has a teacher rather than a god as its focus.

Finally, does religion just depend on the interpretations of the person who makes the judgement?

In sociology, the answers to these questions are quite complicated and depend largely on the school of thought from which the sociologist comes. Some theorists describe religion in a broad sense, allowing in quasi-religions in which groups meet, such as sports fans, union members or others who share values and act in accordance with them. Others prefer a narrower definition which emphasises the significance of more orthodox features, such as prayer, **ritual**, doctrine and mystical forces.

Activity
1 Write down a list of at least 15 keywords or ideas that you associate with the word 'religion'.
2 Complete the following sentence in less than 20 words: 'Religion is…'
Compare your definition with other students and discuss the similarities and differences between them. Take it in turns to write your definitions onto a large sheet of paper and then write a group definition. If you are working on your own, look up and compare several dictionary definitions.

Study point

Do you think that a non-religious person find it easier to study religion objectively than a religious person?

- **Edward Tylor** proposed a minimum definition of religion. He saw religion as 'the belief in Spiritual Beings'.
- **Melford Spiro** defined religion as 'an institution consisting of culturally patterned interaction with culturally postulated superhuman beings'.
- **Paul Radin** said that religion consisted of feelings, acts, customs, and also beliefs associated with feeling. The beliefs had to do with supernatural beings regarded as more powerful than humans, and exercising control of the world. Religious feeling originated in the struggle for existence under conditions of physical and social insecurity. It was a response to fear.

THERE ARE 5,000 DRUIDS IN THE UK, AND THE MOVEMENT ORIGINATED BETWEEN BC 5000-3000. WOULD DRUIDISM BE BETTER DEFINED AS A CULT MOVEMENT OR A RELIGION? (SEE P 69)

The problem with these definitions is that not all religions involve belief in a supernatural or superhuman being.

- **Emile Durkheim** made a distinction between the **sacred** and the **profane**. He said that religion is 'a unified system of beliefs and practices relative to sacred things'. The advantage of this definition is that it recognises the relationship between religious practice and belief; it does not suggest the need for a belief in a single God; and it reminds us of the distinctions between the mystical and the secular, non-spiritual world. However, critics have suggested that his definition is too broad. It suggests that almost any organised belief system which has a mystical element can be classified as religious.

- **Milton Yinger** described non-typical religious belief systems as 'functional equivalents'. They could include beliefs in science, communism, nationalism, humanism and psychoanalysis. He wrote:

---

the alternative to religion may not be some social movement ... but a private pattern of belief and ritual used by an unhappy individual in his attempts to counter personal failure and isolation.

- **Peter Berger** and **Thomas Luckmann** suggested that religion is the outcome of human beings transcending their biological nature to construct a moral world which has meaning and relevance. It becomes a sacred canopy or shield against the random and apparently meaningless events which make life so hazardous.
- **Steve Bruce** pointed out that sociologists have two different ways of defining religion. Functional definitions identify it in terms of what it does (eg, providing solutions to ultimate problems). Substantive definitions identify religion in terms of what it is. For example, beliefs and actions which assume the existence of supernatural powers. His preferred definition is that:

---

religion consists of beliefs, actions and institutions which assume the existence of supernatural entities with powers of action or impersonal powers possessed of moral purpose.

Religion in Modern Britain, 1995

- **Max Weber** was always cautious about providing a specific definition of religion, suggesting that it could only be achieved at the conclusion of a study, when the behaviour of people could be examined to see how far it was influenced by meanings they derived from their understanding or contact with religious institutions or values.

The narrow definitions
- These emphasise the belief in the supernatural: heaven and hell, angels, the devil, miracles.

The broad definitions
- Even culturally based superstitions may be functional in society in the sense that they can provide people with ways of achieving some kind of shared outlook and knowledge about why events happen as they do.

- Any strongly held ideology which structures ideas about the world (such as a belief in communism or in science), could be said to be a secular religion. Even attending a football match might therefore become a functional equivalent of a church service.

THE DIMENSIONS OF RELIGION

Although there is no universally agreed definition of religion, there is an agreement among many sociologists that all religions share a number of core dimensions. The theologian **Ninian Smart** suggested that religions have six dimensions (see below). Some commentators have argued that certain powerful political ideologies, such as Marxism, fascism and conservatism, are quasi-religions. They hold strong rational and emotional appeals and provide people with ultimate answers about how to conduct their lives. Smart attempts to point up the differences in his model, using the dimensions of ritual, myth, doctrine, ethics, social and experiential.

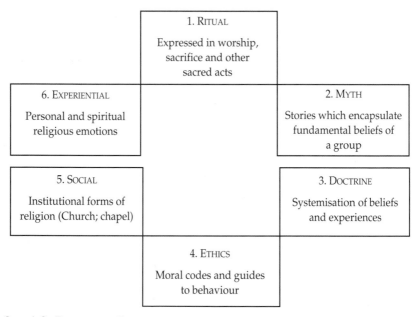

SMART'S SIX DIMENSIONS OF RELIGION
SOURCE: SMART, *THE RELIGIOUS EXPERIENCE OF MANKIND* 1969

The ritual dimension

Rituals are special rites associated with religion. They frequently have connections with the concept of salvation, the creation of purity (as in baptism or ritual bathing, even in dangerously unclean rivers), forgiveness (as in confession) and prayer. Rituals may help to break down barriers between secular and sacred activities. The bull-roarer may: serve as a toy; help round up cattle; or be used as a means of contacting the gods and obtaining spiritual powers.

The mythological dimension

In sociology, a **myth** is a belief about the supernatural. Its truth or falsity is not an issue. Myth does not mean an invented story, but is an aspect of culture and relates to the central ideas of the religion under analysis. Myths may be passed on as stories; eg, the Hindu religion stories in the epic poem, *Mahabharata*, express truths about the religion; in Genesis there are descriptions explaining the possible origin of the world. Some people take myths to be literally true; others see them as ways of expressing religious ideas.

The doctrinal dimension

Religious doctrines are theological statements of belief which are explanations of a structured belief system. They appear in sacred texts as religious principles in all of the major religions:

- In Christianity, it is part of the doctrine that God spoke directly through his son Jesus as described in the Bible.
- In Islam, the doctrines are stated in the Koran.
- In Hinduism, they reflect schools of thought or philosophical interpretations.

It is not unusual to find followers of a religion present different ways of interpreting the doctrines, but the underlying values are upheld.

The ethical dimension

Ethical beliefs are moral codes which the religion provides about how followers *ought* to act. Religions specify acceptable and unacceptable actions, the latter often being subject to special sanctions. In this way religion serves as a source of social control. The Ten Commandments (found in both Judaism and Christianity) set out fundamental ethical rules of behaviour. Some of these are very precise ('thou shalt not kill') and others quite broad ('love thy neighbour'). Hinduism and Buddhism emphasise the ethical value of self control, prohibiting violence, and the importance of truth.

The social dimension

Where religions are established as social institutions (such as the Church of England or Methodism), they become easier to define (see p 64). The membership can be more easily identified. The social dimension is likely to provide a good measure of how religious a society is, by counting heads, although there may be major problems about what constitutes a member and whether they are 'true believers'.

The religious experience dimension

This may be regarded as the most significant dimension; the special experiences of wonder, mystery, reverence and revelation which people report in the relation to religion, are said to be among the specially distinctive qualities. Such experiences can lead to commitment. For example, it may be this which leads on to undertaking a special way of life and to adopt particular ethical patterns of behaviour.

Evaluation

1   It is important to consider how far the dimensions are specifically religious features or whether they could appear equally in a political ideology, for example. These may have equivalent rituals, myths, doctrines, moral codes, social institutions and generate special experiences among members. Many superstitions also involve rituals.

2   Some critics argue that while the first five dimensions above may have such equivalents in other strongly held secular belief systems, the special experience which involvement in religion brings, provides its distinctive character.

3   Other critics are concerned that to provide six key dimensions is to suggest a special order of importance, which might lead to a ranking of different religions in which some exhibit more of the qualities than others. This may discourage the study of some and promote the study of others.

4   Another point to consider is whether there are other dimensions which have been overlooked. Could there equally be an 'artistic and musical dimension'; a 'presence in the community dimension'?

5   Although open to criticism, the six dimensions do help to identify some key features of religion for the purposes of research and enable some distinctions to be made between religion and other types of belief system.

Activity

If available, use the Aspects of Religion CD-ROM to investigate the core dimensions of one world religion. Record your findings in a large table

The core dimensions of ....

Ritual	Myth	Doctrine	Ethics	Social	Experiential

MAGIC

Magic is the attempt to obtain influence with supernatural forces for the benefit of a society or an individual's special ends through non-scientific means. This can include the use of spells, potions, chants, and symbolic rituals. An interest in magic is found in every society, from the most simple and traditional, and where there was little or no access to a scientific understanding, to the most technologically developed.

Nineteenth-century anthropologists (especially Edward Tyler and James Fraser) regarded magic as irrational attempts by 'primitive savages' to control the supernatural world by non-rational means. Malinowski suggested that it was used where technical skills and means were too limited to achieve success in their endeavours. It was found that there were specialist practitioners of magic who could interpret omens, had access to objects with magical properties and could perform the necessary rituals to achieve the desired ends. These practices were concerned with special immediate social problems such as matters of health, weather and crops.

William Goode proposed 11 criteria to distinguish magic from religion:

1 Magic is more instrumental, aiming at end results of a concrete and material kind.
2 Its goals are specific and limited.
3 It is more manipulative in its techniques.
4 It is directed at individual rather than at group goals.
5 It is more a matter of private practice than a group activity.
6 It is more susceptible to substitution of techniques – if one does not work, another is tried.
7 It involves less emotion.
8 Its practice is less obligatory.
9 It is less tied to specific times and occasions.
10 It is potentially more anti-social.
11 It takes less supernatural forms.

Peter Worsley suggested that magic is logical within the cultural understanding of the people concerned. He described the emergence of 'Cargo Cults', in which attempts were made by the islanders to induce the arrival of more valuable goods or cargoes onto their shores by magical means. This resulted from the experience of some tribal people on whose lands ships carrying valuable goods had been wrecked. Where the cargoes had come from or who had sent them, the tribal people did not know. Subsequent attempts to obtain more by means of charms and rituals was, in a sense, a perfectly logical procedure, since they did not have access to the technological knowledge to explain their origin. Worsley argued that it may be a mistaken view to assume that people in primitive societies were any better informed of the origins of their religious traditions than people in modern industrial societies.

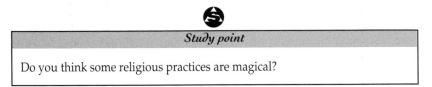

Study point
Do you think some religious practices are magical?

SUPERSTITION

Large numbers of people in modern industrial societies believe in superstition. (See table 2a.) Superstition implies the existence of an unseen and unknown mysterious force which can influence a person's life for good or ill. There are no special practitioners, no sacred or other specialist books. Those who are superstitious usually have difficulty in identifying the source of power which is being influenced, and can seldom specify for how long the ill or good luck lasts before the omen can be forgotten (except perhaps in the case of a broken mirror). Superstition is generally concerned with:

- seeking to control short-term matters relating to daily life, and frequently (but not exclusively) it operates on a personal level, rather than a communal one.
- interpreting observed phenomena which may be omens (does the black cat bring good or bad luck?).
- understanding and performing rituals to influence the outcome of an event and to combat the potential ill effects of bad omens (eg, throwing a portion of spilt salt over a shoulder, avoiding ladders, holding lucky charms).

These widely held superstitious/magical beliefs have become known as subterranean theologies to distinguish them from more orthodox religious belief systems. Sociologists are interested in these beliefs because they appear to challenge the idea that society is becoming more secular. They are seen as proof that many people in modern industrial societies still make use of mystical beliefs in their daily lives. They usually involve:

- an irrational fear of the unknown and lack of control of their own destiny
- a strong emotional component, which affects behaviour and can be observed in their actions
- an acceptance of unusual beliefs frequently justified as ancient lore.

Table 2a: *Superstitions held by British people in 1991 (%)*			
PROPOSITION	DEFINITELY AND PROBABLY TRUE	PROBABLY AND DEFINITELY FALSE	NO ANSWER CAN'T CHOOSE
Good luck charms sometimes bring good luck	22	72	6
Some fortune tellers can foresee the future	40	53	8
Some faith healers have God-given powers	45	45	10
A person's star sign at birth (horoscope) can influence the course of their future life	28	64	9

Table 2b: *People who believe in God (%)*	
PROPOSITION	(%)
I don't believe in God	10
I believe in a higher power of some kind	13
I believe in God some of the time	13
I have some doubts, but I do believe in God	26
I have no doubts that God exists	23
I don't know	2

SOURCE: BRITISH SOCIAL ATTITUDE SURVEY 1991.

Study point

In about 100–150 words draw out some significant points from tables 2a and 2b with regard to belief in superstition and in God.

Activity

Read the following extract. Do you agree or disagree with the surgeons' suggestion? Explain your answer.

An apparently healthy middle-aged woman, mother of five children, was admitted in March 1965 to a hospital in Canada for a minor operation. This was straightforward and went as expected, the woman regaining consciousness before leaving the theatre. An hour later she suddenly collapsed, and in spite of every effort by the doctors died the following morning. Post-mortem examination revealed extensive haemorrhage mainly of the adrenal glands, without any other pathology that might explain it. Later the surgeons were informed that she had been to a fortune-teller at the age of five, who had told her that she would die at the age of forty-three; her forty-third birthday was one week before the operation, and she had told her sister and one of the nurses that she did not expect to survive it. The surgeons suggested the prophesy may have indirectly caused her fatality. They said 'the severe emotional tensions of this patient superimposed on the physiological stress of surgery may have had a bearing upon her death'.

Jahoda, The Psychology of Superstition (1969)

Natural scientists do not deal with mystical or supernatural events because they cannot be observed or measured, although some parapsychology experiments are sometimes undertaken to try to resolve questions about sensory perception, telepathy and other related issues. Sociologists frequently aim to adopt scientific procedures to test theories about patterns of religious belief and behaviour.

Activity

Read the following extract and then answer these questions:

1 Explain how the effect of the power of prayer on hospital patients is being scientifically tested.
2 Outline the strengths and weaknesses of Professor Stannard's experiment.
3 Discuss whether religious phenomena such as prayer can be tested scientifically. Explain your answer.

Professor Russell Stannard, a Christian and a scientist, is about to undertake a study in three American hospitals over a two year period, to examine the power of prayer on patients. He will use scientific procedures. The study is being funded by an organisation aimed at the progress of religion and will involve three groups of 600 patients. Two groups will be told that they may be prayed for by a special praying team. In fact one will be prayed for, the other will not. Neither group, however, will know which is which. A third group will know that they are being prayed for and will be checked to see whether the knowledge has any psychosomatic effects on their symptoms and progress. Professor Stannard acknowledged that a result showing no significant differences between the groups would not necessarily prove that prayer did not help, because people might pray for themselves, or be prayed for by family and friends.

Adapted from an article by Matthew Brace, The Independent, April 11th 1997

WHY DOES THE SUPERNATURAL REMAIN ATTRACTIVE?

Those who criticise the influence of the mystical in modern life, are described as Rationalists. Yet surveys show that 28 per cent of British people believe that a person's horoscope can predict their future lives; 9 per cent think it may have an effect. Astrology columns are found in broadsheet newspapers and many expensive glossy magazines; *The Times Literary Supplement* featured a full review of astrology books; *The X-Files Book of the Unexplained* was a bestseller for more than 32 weeks; television devotes many hours a week to such programmes because they are exceptionally popular.

In an article for *The Guardian* in 1996, **Catherine Bennett** examined some possible explanations for such belief systems and the criticisms which have been raised against them. She argued that irrationality cuts across classes and has many significant dangers. She noted that when the geneticist Richard Dawkins wrote an article in *The Independent* earlier that year, stating that astrology is an affront to both aesthetics and truth, he had extensive responses (an entire page) attacking his views, from its largely middle class readership. In her analysis she cites the work of:

- **Nicholas Humphrey** says that 'scientific materialism is regarded by many, even by some of its prophets, as deeply unsatisfying: scary, bewildering, insulting, demeaning, dispiriting, confining'. He suggests that people want 'to get their souls back from science'.
- **Gilbert Murray** believes that superstition thrives on uncertainty in a society 'in which the fortunes of people seem to bear practically no relation to their merits or efforts'.

Bennett also notes the many critics of such material. It is their argument that once a rational process of living is lost, people are open to all kinds of manipulation by anyone with a vested interest in controlling or frightening them into particular ways of behaving.

- The author of *Antiquities of the Common People* (1725) said that 'the Observations of omens, such as falling salt, a hare crossing the way etc are sinful and diabolical'. These caused people to become 'the slaves of a superstition'.

- **Keith Thomas** wrote that even 300 years ago,

---

astrology had ceased in all but the unsophisticated circles, to be regarded either as science or a crime: it had become simply a joke ... but why should anyone have believed it in the first place? To our eyes the notion that the daily life of human beings should be determined by the motions of the heavenly bodies seems so fantastic that it is difficult to understand how men of intelligence and perspicacity could ever have accepted it.

He concluded that now, the intellectual vitality of the subject was gone for ever.

Superstitions are not always harmless (see Activities, pp 15–16). Some practitioners of unproven alternative therapies appear to be profiting from the movement away from scientific based medicine. A professor of surgery at the Royal Marsden hospital has said:

---

people drive cars, fly in aeroplanes, enjoy the comfort of a house, designed by architects who understand geometry and physics. Yet they are seduced by antique philosophies, which are seductive in their simplicity.

Activity
Look at the mysteries in table 3 and decide whether they include religious, magical, superstitious or scientific beliefs. Select some and discuss how they may or may not be open to scientific test.

Table 3: *Examples of mysteries*	
Astrology	Fairies
UFOs and aliens	Witchcraft
Ghosts	Extra sensory perception (ESP)
The Loch Ness Monster	Faith Healing
Voodoo	Alternative Medicine
Standing stones (eg Stonehenge)	Predestination
Big Foot	Ouija board predictions
Telepathy	Fire walking
Fortune telling & Tarot cards	Spontaneous human combustion
The Bermuda Triangle	Near death experiences

SUMMARY

There can be no single definition of religion. Each may contain some common themes and many differences. Research shows that patterns of mystical belief develop differently in different societies, where they also change and evolve. Sociologists examine them in terms of

- the functions they serve
- their possible dysfunctions for the society
- the ways in which they can be distinguished according to the values and ideals they offer
- the effects they have on the people and institutions of the societies in which they appear, especially in relations to the family, class, politics, and economic issues.

It is apparent that there are great problems in distinguishing religion from superstition and magic. In some cultures they are closely bound together. In others, where there is a tradition of theological and philosophical investigation, attempts are made to establish theoretical differences. Sociologists develop models or typologies to try to show what these differences and similarities are, so that research can be undertaken and a process of categorisation follow. However, as far as people are concerned, even the truly religious person can also be found to engage in superstitious practices in their daily lives .

STUDY GUIDES

Group work

1 In small groups, discuss the issue that even in a highly scientific age, people are prepared to allow the irrational to control part of their lives. Consider the strengths and weaknesses of the ideas expressed. Reach a group consensus (note dissenting views) and present them to the whole group when reconvened. What is the majority view? Does this vary between gender or any other variable?

2 Conduct a study that examines the relationship between superstition and social class, gender or age.

3 Outline the similarities and differences between religion, magic and superstition. Record your answers with examples in a table. Justify and discuss your conclusions.

Key Concepts activity

Each group to define and discuss the terms listed on p 6, with examples from their own experience. Write the definition on a Key Concept Card for revision purposes (see p 3).

Practice questions

1 'Religion is the belief in Spiritual Beings'. Discuss.
2 Can magic, superstition and other types of mystical belief be distinguished from religion, or does religion inevitably contain aspects of such beliefs?
3 'Science and religion are incompatible'. Discuss.

Coursework

1 Explore the meanings which people place on religion in their lives.
2 Examine how people justify being both religious and superstitious. Consider this in terms of people from different occupational, age and gender groups.
3 Undertake an observational study in which you claim to have had various mystical or supernatural experiences.
  a Note the levels of scepticism or acceptance of your claims among those with whom you discuss them. What seems to determine their response?
  b How easy would it be to persuade large numbers of people that you had special insights into the supernatural as a result of your experiences?

3

CLASSICAL SOCIOLOGICAL THEORIES OF RELIGION

Introduction

THIS CHAPTER LOOKS at the classical sociological theories of religion in society. In particular, it examines the ideas of Marx, who stressed the ways in which religion deludes people; the Functionalist Theories of Durkheim, who examined the contribution of religion to social solidarity; and Weber's Action Theory, which explored the way that religion provides meaning for people in an uncertain world and can influence processes of change.

Table 4: *Theorists, concepts and issues in this chapter*			
KEY THEORIST	KEY THEORIES	KEY CONCEPTS	KEY IDEAS
Karl Marx	Marxism	Alienation Class struggle Conflict False consciousness Hegemony Opiate of the people Ruling class	Religion is a source of social control by the ruling class
Emile Durkheim	Functionalism	Anomie Collective conscience Functional alternatives Profane Sacred Social control	Religion is a source of social cohesion and integration

		Socialisation Solidarity Totemism	
Max Weber	Action Theory	Spirit of capitalism Protestant Ethic Charisma Disenchantment Ideal types Legitimation Meaning Rationalisation Theodicy of disprivilege Desacrilisation Authority	Religion can be a source of social change under certain circumstances

MARXISM

Karl Marx (1818–1884) was greatly influenced by the German philosopher Ludwig Feuerbach, who thought that religion was a human construction and described it in terms of myths, in which human characteristics were projected into a non-human realm of existence. From here, men and women could be controlled like puppets, by the gods they had created. For Marx, too, religion appealed to the person:

> *who either has not yet found himself or has already lost himself again ... Man is the world of man, the state, society. This state, this society, produces religion, ... It is the sigh of the oppressed creature, the heart of a heartless world ... It is the opium of the people.*
>
> *Karl Marx, Contribution to the Critique of Hegel's Philosophy of Right, 1844*

He believed that people become alienated (detached from each other as their lives are determined by forces beyond their control) as a result of an exploitative economic system, in which capitalism dehumanises and divides people through the processes of class inequalities. Religion emerges as a product of alienation, in which people endeavour to regain some illusory purpose and an acceptance of their lot. The reality is that religion is a drug to make their unhappy lot bearable. They are unable to see the disturbing realities of the deceptions which control their lives. It is therefore the product of a class society.

CONFLICT THEORY

Marxism is also referred to as **conflict structural theory**; this is the idea that society has a structure, which is the outcome of past actions by people who have established the socially accepted ways of doing things, which become normative patterns of behaviour. Sometimes conflicts arise when changes are made to the structures and organisations, and groups emerge to oppose or defend the changes.

The conflict structuralist starts with idea that people have needs to be satisfied (food, clothing and shelter). The political and economic structures determine how these are met and resources shared. The analysis suggests that the resources are inevitably shared unequally because power is held by a minority of rich people in whose interest the economy operates. This leads to exploitation and oppression by the ruling class, who impose an ideology on the oppressed groups, which inhibits their chances of seeing the true facts about their lives. For example, religious values of suffering and acceptance are used to inhibit action by the oppressed. These are epitomised in biblical pronouncements, such as 'The meek shall inherit the earth'; 'Blessed are the poor'. To express anger at their current position is to show unacceptable anger against God. In this way, religion diverts revolutionary uprisings and other social discontent.

Marx concludes that religion will and should be abolished, then the illusion it creates would disappear. Like his predecessor Feuerbach, he wanted to 'allow the unclouded light of truth to stream in upon us'. He suggested there would be no place for false ideologies such as religion in his socialist utopia; people would then be living in heaven on earth.

Study points

1   Marx believed that religion was an instrument of social control. Identify and describe three ways in which religion acts as a form of social control in contemporary society.
2   How do you think a Marxist sociologist would interpret this statement from a letter of St. James (2: 1–5): 'God chose the poor to be the heirs to the kingdom'?
3   How might they deal with a statement from the same letter, in which he says 'Do not combine faith in Jesus Christ with the making of distinctions between classes of people; if you see a rich man and give him the best seat and tell the poor man to sit on the floor, can't you see that you have turned yourself into a corrupt judge?'

POINTS TO SUPPORT MARX

1   The caste system of traditional India has relied on Hindu religious beliefs to justify and maintain the values of caste discrimination, occupation and social patterns of acceptable behaviour.
2   In Medieval Europe, monarchs ruled their kingdoms by the divine right of kings (chosen by God).

3 Religion continues to legitimate many events in modern society; eg Parliament starts each day with prayers; monarchs are crowned in cathedrals.

4 Slavery in the United States was often defended on religious grounds. For example, in 1700 Judge Saffin of Boston wrote:

> *The Order that God hath set in the world, who have Ordained different degrees and orders of men, some to the High and Honourable, some to the Low and Despicable ... yea, some to be born slaves, and so to remain during their lives, as hath been proved.*
>
> *(Montagu, 1964)*

5 Afrikaners of South Africa justified their policy of apartheid on religious grounds.

6 Religion has traditionally remained strong among immigrant groups who may be among the economically poorest members of a society.

CRITICISMS OF MARX

- Marx used an evolutionary model of social development which has been discredited. According to his model, societies passed through a series of stages or epochs which were each characterised by a particular mode of production. These changed from a primitive form of communism, to ancient society (relying on slavery), then to feudal society (which made use of a body of serfs), to modern capitalism, which required a small number of owners and a large number of workers. The final stage (also discredited in recent years) was that of communism, when there would be a fully free, non-religious society. Mankind would then enter into an earthly heaven.

- Some critics have suggested that Marxism is itself another 'functional alternative' to religion. It offers insights about the world, prescriptions for ways of improving it; sacred (Marxist) texts; an inspired prophet of change; a well thought-out ideology for believers to adopt, with the promise of final salvation if his ideas are followed exactly.

- Max Weber opposed a Marxist view. He showed how religious values had a major effect on transforming the economic structure of society, promoting major changes rather than inhibiting them. See p 33.

- There are examples of priests and other theologians taking a very revolutionary stance, based on their interpretations of religious doctrines. In the 1960s and 1970s, many American clergy were active in the movement to end the war in Vietnam. Religious leaders have made important contributions towards increased racial equality in the United States, eg Martin Luther King, Jr. is a Baptist minister. Pro-democracy demonstrators in Kenya in 1997 included religious ministers.

• In this century, some critics have argued that Marx overstated the ways in which the ruling class used religion as a tool of control. They argue that the real power of the ruling class is in their wealth, their social contacts and the related networks which enable them to survive as a class.

Activity

Write a definition of each of the following key concepts using the words which follow to help you:

• **Alienation**: capitalist organisation; separation; deprivation; dehumanising
• **Class struggle**: conflict; owners of the means of production; revolution
• **Conflict**: the powerless; class interests; historical inevitability
• **False consciousness**: accept the world; ideological power; delusion
• **Hegemony**: power; imposed values; power elites; dominant ideology
• **Historical materialism**: social progress; economic forces; class conflicts
• **Liberation theology**: belief in opposing oppression; Catholic theologians
• **Opiate of the people**: capitalist societies; oppressed classes; delusion
• **Ruling class**: power elites; exploitation; control; wealth
• **Social control**: conformity; dominant values; sanctions; norms.

FUNCTIONALISM

Functionalism is sometimes referred to as **structural** theory, **consensus** theory or **systems** theory. A sociologist who adopts a functionalist perspective investigates how the parts, structures or systems of society are interrelated; eg, how the educational system is connected to the economic, religious, and family systems. This involves undertaking research to establish the major parts of the institutions, isolating variables and determining how they function. Functionalists hold that society functions in a similar way to the human body. If one part of the body fails (such as the heart) then it will have a major effect on other parts (the brain, the limbs and ultimately the life of the person). In this way, religion contributes to the survival needs of a society. Distinctions are made between:

• **Functional prerequisites** – the institutions which must exist if that society is to survive over time; religion functions to achieve social solidarity and value consensus
• **Functional alternatives** – structures which can produce similar ends, such as the integration of people into a community through membership of a large association, rather than a church
• **Manifest functions** – which produce intended consequences
• **Latent functions** – consequences which are not intended
• **Dysfunctions** – factors which inadvertently work against the intended aim.

EXAMPLE

The Zulus of South East Africa held a ceremony to celebrate the goddess of crop fertility. During the ceremony the women took over the jobs, clothes and behaviour of men, who remained confined in their huts.

The manifest function:
To please the goddess, ensuring a successful harvest.

The latent function:
To act as a safety valve for the frustrations of women, who lead a hard and difficult life with an inferior status to that of men. The reversal of roles expresses their frustrations. The result is to maintain the stability of the social order.

Possible dysfunctional features:
If the society underwent rapid technological change, the custom may be so entrenched that it inhibits effective social and economic development of adaptation to new circumstances, and so promotes disharmony.

THE FUNCTIONS OF RELIGION

According to Tischler et al, religion performs a number of important social functions:

1 It brings people together physically which promotes social cohesion.
2 It reaffirms the group's beliefs and values.
3 It helps maintain norms, mores and prohibitions so that violation of a secular law – murder or incest for instance – is also a violation of the religious code and may warrant ritual punishment or purification.
4 It transmits a group's cultural heritage from one generation to the next.
5 It offers emotional support to individuals during times of stress and at important stages in their life cycle, such as puberty, marriage and death.

Activity

Working in small groups:

1   Discuss Tischler's five functions of religion. Can these functions be fulfilled by another institution in contemporary society?
2   Suggest how these functions are achieved by religion in contemporary society.

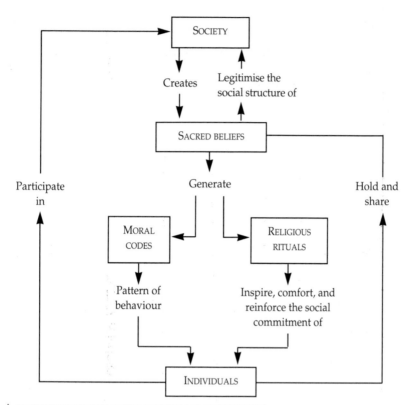

A FUNCTIONALIST VIEW OF SOCIETY, RELIGION AND THE INDIVIDUAL
SOURCE: TISCHLER ET AL 1986

EMILE DURKHEIM [1858 – 1917]

Durkheim contributed greatly to the development of functionalism. Although not a religious person, he made an analysis of the religious practices of Australian Aborigines, whom he took to be an example of the most primitive people of that time. He was interested to establish how social order was created and maintained in a society, and his conclusion was that religion was the source of all harmonious social life.

ASPECTS OF DURKHEIM'S THOUGHT

The Elementary Forms of the Religious Life (1912)

Durkheim opposed the materialist views of Marx. However, he also rejected the idea that religion must involve a belief in deities or spirits, and said that religion is a universal human institution which permeates all aspects of life. While the effects may vary between societies, in some it may influence choice of name, diet, music, art, calendar and concepts of time. He said that

> *Religion is something eminently social. Religious representations are collective representations which express collective realities; the rites are a manner of acting which take rise in the midst of the assembled group which are destined to excite, maintain or recreate mental states in these groups.*

The Sacred and Profane

Durkheim defined religion as 'a unified system of beliefs and practices relative to sacred things set apart and forbidden'. He distinguished between the sacred and the profane (non-sacred or secular aspects of social life).

- **Sacred things.** These are divine not just on practical grounds, but because of some special qualities they possess. For example, a river (Ganges); a place (Bethlehem, Mecca, Amritsar); a book, (The Koran, Bhagavad-Gita, Torah, Bible); a person (Buddha, Mohammed, Jesus); an object or animal (the aboriginal bull-roarer; a crucifix; a cow); a day or period of time (Easter, Divali, Eid, Passover and Visakha). They have become invested over time with a sense of awe and holy significance.
- **Sacred ceremonies.** These draw people together for community activity and a sense of protection. They may involve singing and dancing, prayer and ritual. The emotional involvement is a pleasurable thing which spreads through the group. In some circumstances there may be an intense feeling of magical powers.
- **Sacred places.** These are places where special rites occurred in earlier times and the objects used became invested with spiritual significance.

Totemism

Durkheim analysed what he thought was the most primitive and simple form of religion known to man. **Totemism** (the practice of worshipping a natural object known as a totem) was practised by Australian Aboriginal tribes. He found that each Aboriginal clan is represented by a sacred symbol known as a totem. This is an ordinary object, usually an element of the natural world such as a particular species of bird, animal or plant, or feature of the landscape, that is imbued with sacred qualities. It is often regarded as a helper or guardian spirit with supernatural powers and is deeply respected and venerated. Indeed, it is carved on the bull-roarer which is the most sacred object in Aboriginal ritual.

Durkheim believed that religious symbols such as totems, as well as religion itself, arose from within society, not outside it. The totem symbolised both supernatural powers and the social life of the clan. The rites associated with the sacred totems and the mystical sense (known as mana) they evoked, represent the elementary forms of religious life. The clearly visible totem became the means of objectifying the otherwise invisible social life of the group. When the clan members took part in religious worship, involving rituals, rites and ceremonies using sacred objects such as bull-roarers and totems, they were really worshipping and revering their own society which the objects represented. He concluded that a central function of religion for the Aboriginals is to give clan members a symbol of group life around which their community can unite.

THE FUNCTIONS OF RELIGION

1 **Stability and cohesion** – shared religion binds people closely together.
   a Religion forms a balanced and cohesive moral community. It is a means of protecting individuals from anomie, alienation and the threats of disruptive mass movements, and so maximises the individual's potential for happiness.
   b Shared religious experiences provide the social cement for group unity and consensus.

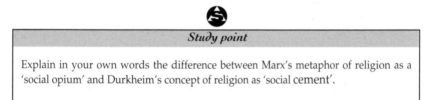

Study point

Explain in your own words the difference between Marx's metaphor of religion as a 'social opium' and Durkheim's concept of religion as 'social cement'.

2 **Social identity** – shared religion gives people an identity and social membership.
   a This is achieved through special naming ceremonies, in christening and baptism in the Christian church. For Durkheim, group solidarity is affirmed and heightened during collective ceremony and ritual.
   b They represent the necessary power of the social group over the otherwise isolated, anomic individual.
   c Religion serves to integrate the person into the society. It is functionally useful for people to grow up identifying with a particular place or nation, to strengthen a person's sense of national commitment, especially if either religion or nation come under threat.
3 **Collective conscience** – religion unites people in moral ways.
   a The group affirms its belief in the central values through its commitment to the religious system. These sentiments produce 'value consensus'.
   b Religion thereby generates and maintains the collective conscience. This was observable in its effects and was open to scientific study just as other

social facts could be studied and analysed, by collecting relevant statistics, through careful observation and recording or other experimental methods.

c   Durkheim saw society as a moral community, whose members were socialised into accepting appropriate patterns of behaviour over time. This is an unending process since people are always being integrated into new groups, adopting new norms, absorbing new values and adapting new patterns of behaviour.

d   An orderly social life is only possible when people share moral values; in this way, society becomes embedded in the individual.

4   **Socialisation and social control** – religion represents the value system of the society.

a   It is a conservative force which contributes to moral and wider social order and stability.

b   Many cultural norms are given sacred legitimacy by religious beliefs, eg the Ten Commandments provide a prescription for an orderly lifestyle. By promoting such values through family, school and church, the process of socialisation occurs.

c   Appropriate modes of thinking and behaving are controlled in ways which will promote the good, orderly society.

5   **Meaning and purpose** – religion gives meaning and purpose to people's lives.

a   In the face of death, disease, and the hazards of everyday living, people are vulnerable to all kinds of disasters beyond their control. Religious beliefs offer people comfort in times of crisis.

b   It is the institution which gives people the strength to continue, and promotes the long-term maintenance of society as a result.

Study point
How far do you think support for a football team may be seen as a functional alternative to religion?

POINTS OF EVALUATION: STRENGTHS OF DURKHEIM'S THEORY

1   The functionalists helped to reestablish interest in the analysis of religion. They put it into a wider social context, to see its relations with other institutions in society. Later theorists (such as Merton) developed additional concepts, such as those of manifest functions, dysfunctions and functional alternatives; so that science, nationalism, communism and even football, might be seen as serving as a functional religious alternative for some.

2   Durkheim's work is accepted as a brilliant sociological account. He showed the inadequacies of earlier approaches and produced a more elaborate explanation.

This laid emphasis on the importance of establishing the origin of religion, which he saw as the worship of society itself in group rituals and ceremonies.

3 He demonstrated how the collective features of religious activity are crucially important for the members and for the society in providing stability and integration. The functions of ritual were to assert the power of society over the individuals who comprised it, and so maintain the social solidarity of the social group. Religion was not a vague fear of the unknown forces which surrounded them, but a relationship between members of a community who needed institutions to protect its moral and long term social life.

CRITICISMS OF DURKHEIM

1 Durkheim's analysis was of small traditional societies. His ideas have been criticised as being inappropriate to complex modern societies. Evans-Pritchard argued that there is no evidence that totemism arose in the way Durkheim speculated that it did, or that other religions are ultimately derived from it.

2 He made use of ideas which were rather mysterious and difficult to prove in a scientific way. The collective consciousness of the group, their social mind, was described as the source of religion; it is hard to prove that every religious system is indispensable for the maintenance of the whole society. If a religious group abandons its presence in a society, it makes no significant difference.

3 Although he accepted that as a response to wider social changes, scientific thinking will increasingly replace religious explanation, he did not consider religion from a dysfunctional point of view.

   a Some religious movements may advocate revolutionary activity and others the maintenance of class divisions. For example, during the Middle Ages, religious beliefs motivated European Christians to organise the Crusades against Muslims in the East.

   b In Northern Ireland religious identities have resulted in disharmony; in the southern states of USA, the reactionary Ku Klux Klan movement has a religious basis; in recent years there have been great divisions between clergy over secular and theological issues which have led to acrimony.

   c In the 1990s there have been unresolved debates about whether or not the Prince of Wales should, in a multi-cultural society, be described as Defender of Faith, when he ascends to the throne.

Activity
Give a five minute multi-media presentation to the rest of your group on 'The Functionalist Approach to Religion'. Use illustrations, OHP, diagrams, religious background music, examples of sacred totems; suggest a group activity.

SOCIAL ACTION THEORY

MAX WEBER (1864–1920)

Weber adopted an influential **social action approach** that social behaviour is best understood by examining the meaning which people as social actors place on events and ideas. Their actions are directed by the interpretations they make, and their response to religion is important in shaping a view of the world. People can establish and justify reasons for actions, and so make sense of the world.

Weber argues that ideas will only have significance in the long term if they meet the material interests of particular social groups. It is when both the significant values and the special interests are present that a transformation in social structures can take place.

Study point

To what extent do you think religion still provides meaning and structure to people in contemporary society? Give examples and consider the alternatives to which some people turn.

THEODICY OF PRIVILEGE OR NON-PRIVILEGE

Weber established a perspective and analysis of religion in which he examined its role in relation to the economic systems of society. He describes religion as the attempt to make sense of people's fortunes and the apparently random effects of day-to-day life. Religion is able to resolve social tensions by providing explanations for the apparently unfair patterns of life; eg, for why the good person often achieves less than the malicious and unpleasant person; why highly valued members of society die young. Weber calls this the **theodicy of privilege or non-privilege**.

In his analysis, Weber examines the relationship between different social groups, the values, beliefs and aspirations they hold, and their consequences for the ways the society develops over time. He argues that a person's life chances are directly related to the wider social groups of which they are a member. These class or status groups hold different positions according to the ways in which they are valued in the society. Such groups will tend to have different patterns of religious values. For some, the small strict sect is more attractive than the High Church; for others, the chapel is more appropriate than the Catholic Church and so on. Such ideas are shaped within groups by their expectations and their experiences. Weber is interested in the ways in which groups are infected by and become carriers of the ideas.

RATIONALITY

The concept of **rationality** is used to explain why western culture developed in different ways from those in the east. In the west, the scientific method became established, leading to advances in technology and industry, accompanied by the growth of rational bureaucratic organisations. There is no value judgement being made that one is superior to the other; they simply display differences in development.

RELIGION AND SOCIAL CHANGE

Weber demonstrated how the different religious ethics led to different economic outcomes. The more meditational religions of the east had different economic consequences to the puritanical Protestant religions of the west (which advocated hard industrious work, a conscientious approach to life, and the appropriate good deeds to accompany it, as a means of salvation).

He also showed that other great world religions were not suited to the development of capitalism. Buddhism, Hinduism, Islam and Catholicism did not develop the necessary economic rational values to promote skills in financial occupations in the way that Calvinistic Protestantism did. In this way he showed how religious values and ideals can promote and encourage social change rather than oppose it. Religion is not, therefore, a necessarily 'conservative force' in the ways that Marx and Durkheim suggested.

Later Weberians note how religious ideas can influence and introduce intended and unintended changes in the social structure. In some cases religious ideals have been used as a force for radical change:

- Capitalism was the unintended outcome of specific religious meanings and motives.
- In the Irish Republic there is an association of the Catholic Church with Republicanism.
- In South Africa, the anti-apartheid movement was led by Archbishop Desmond Tutu.
- In Poland, the Catholic Church supported the Solidarity Movement in the 1980s which eventually led to the overthrow of the Communist regime. Revolutionary groups sometimes have close contacts with religious leaders, who share similar ideals, making use of religion in their attempts to overthrow the existing social structure.
- Hindu leaders were effective in removing British rule from India by appealing to religious ideals.

THE PROTESTANT ETHNIC AND THE SPIRIT OF CAPITALISM

John Calvin (1509–64) was a French Protestant reformer and the founder of Calvinism. He said faith must be based on scripture alone. Weber argued that there was a clear connection between the religious ideals enshrined in Calvin's doctrines and the 'spirit of capitalism'. Unlike Lutheranism, which preached that people must follow their calling, Calvinism did not teach that people must stay in the social class into which they were born. Weber accepted that Calvinism was not the single cause in the development of capitalism; there were many other relevant factors, (including the availability of a suitable work force and appropriate technological skills) but nonetheless, the beliefs they provided were significant contributory factors.

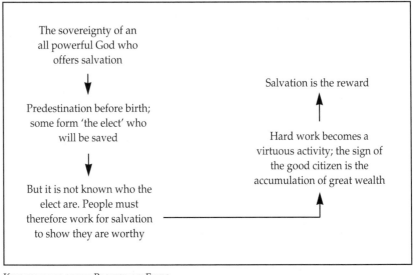

KEYS FEATURES OF THE PROTESTANT ETHIC

Study point

Explain and discuss the statements below.

'The Godly and hardworking man shall have prosperity, but he that follows pleasures shall have much sorrow'

John Brown, a 16th century Protestant merchant

> *'Even if you are called to the poorest labouring job, do not complain because it is wearisome, nor imagine that God thinks any less of you. But cheerfully follow it, and make it your pleasure and joy that you are still in your heavenly master's services, though it be the lowest thing.'*
>
> *Richard Baxter, a 17th century English Puritan*

Jary and Jary summarised the key ideas of Calvinism; they claim it:

1 moulded a type of character ideally suited to expanding the system
2 legitimated individualistic profit-seeking by making it a duty willed by God
3 legitimated the division of labour by making specialist occupational activity a duty
4 legitimated capitalist exploitation and work discipline by making conscientious labour a duty
5 created a cultural climate in which poverty could be seen as a result of individual moral failings, such as idleness and thriftiness, and so freed the system, for responsibility of poverty.

Study point

Do you agree with Weber's idea that religion promotes and encourages major changes in the organisation of a society? Consider the examples of Iran and Israel where religion is of great importance in national life.

LEGITIMATION

Legitimacy is the morally accepted right of one person (such as a priest), organisation (such as a church) or group (such as a class) to exert significant control over another person or group. Societies develop formulas for transmitting the nature of the legitimacy so that each generation can become subject to it and to the sanctions that sustain it. To maintain power the holders must be accepted as a legitimate, so that the values, rules and judgements laid down are seen as just and valid. Weber identified three ideal types of legitimate authority:

1 Hereditary authority, such as a king or leader – obedience is based on the fact that this is what has always been the case
2 Rational-legal authority – the official is elected and therefore deserves obedience
3 Charismatic authority – the leader is popular and has personality characteristics which result in devotion and dedication to the cause s/he espouses, and the promises are attractive.

The charismatic leader

Much religious change and development has tended to take the form of rather sudden innovation brought about by exceptional **charismatic** leaders or prophets. Hamilton has suggested that Weber believed the charismatic prophet was one of the most important figures in religious history, an agent of social change. In contrast, the priest represents tradition.

Examples of charismatic leaders include Jesus Christ, John Wesley, John Calvin, Desmond Tutu, Billy Graham, Ayatollah Khomeini, Sun Myung Mood, David Koresh, Malcolm X, Bhagwan Shree Rajneesh, Ghandi, Martin Luther King, Jr.

Weber examined the ways in which power was maintained in a society, and the sources of its legitimacy. He regarded religion as a valuable source of such legitimation for those seeking to justify their power. Parkin notes that 'he went so far as to say that for some this was the only or principal purpose of religion'. He is suggesting that membership of a powerful religious group can provide an individual with a valuable moral qualification to justify his economic activity.

DISENCHANTMENT AND DESACRILISATION

Weber predicts that as a society becomes more rational in organisation and values, its religious views and practices lose significance. He describes this as a process of **disenchantment** with the modern world. Science begins to provide answers to questions which were once mysterious and given supernatural explanations. Rational, reasoned analysis produces the meaning and understanding which people seek. The loss of the sacred, in which supernatural forces play little role in society, is the process of **desacrilisation**.

EVALUATION

Strengths of Weber's theory

1 Weber presented a critical alternative to the economic determinism of Marx.
2 He saw religion as a force for social change.
3 He successfully examined the relationship between the economic position of people in the society and their religious beliefs in ways that had not been undertaken before.
4 He was less concerned with the moral or ethical teachings of religious leaders, and was more interested in the ways in which the ideas they taught passed into the culture and shaped day-to-day behaviour.
5 He was very concerned with the problem of meaning. This concern has been examined by later writers adopting his perspective, who have argued that it is religion which helps people construct their reality, make sense of the world around them and gain some protection from the forces which can destroy or undermine their normal sense of stability. Weber showed how it can play a

legitimating role in providing the answers to questions about problems relating to birth, life, and death.

6 He undertook what has been described as a monumental historical-comparative research programme: Boudon and Bourricaud have said

---

'the Weberian heritage has furnished a series of continually relevant landmarks to those researchers who have not given up the association of both a wide-ranging historical-comparative perspective with careful institutional analysis and personal commitment with methodological detachment'.

Boudon and Bourricand (1989)

---

7 Sociologists who have adopted Weber's approach have now probably become the most dominant and influential theorists on religion. His work has become influential in the analysis of the beliefs and membership of sects and in the relationship between class and religious affiliation.

Criticisms

1 Sombart argued that Weber misinterpreted Calvinistic traditions and beliefs. He suggested that Calvinism was against profit for its own sake, although Weber saw this as an unintended consequence and said that there was evidence that this was how Protestants did behave.

2 Samuelsson and Tawney have questioned Weber's claim that Calvinism preceded capitalism. They argue that countries such as Switzerland, Scotland, Hungary and parts of Holland all contained Calvinistic populations but did not develop capitalism until relatively much later. Also, capitalist enterprises were well underway in Catholic countries such as Italy, Belgium and Germany before the Protestant Reformation. However Hamilton argues that this criticism ignores Weber's clear statement that many other conditions are required for capitalism to emerge and flourish, not just the appropriate motivations stimulated by Protestantism.

3 Trevor-Roper argues that it was not the religious doctrines of Calvinism that contributed to the development of capitalism. He believes that nonconformist Calvinists devoted themselves to innovative and specialised business activities because they were excluded from traditional occupations by law.

4 Parkin suggests that Weber overemphasises Calvinist teachings which are generally compatible with the capitalist ethos, while he discounted or underplayed those elements which appear to undermine his arguments. Where other religions are concerned, he may have adopted the opposite approach.

Activity

Using a large sheet of paper present Weber's approach to religion in diagram or 'mind map' form. Use the concepts from p 22.

SUMMARY

Marx, Durkheim and Weber present the classical analysis of religion, and all have been influential.

Karl Marx:

- pointed to the relativity of religious ideas and ethical value judgements associated with them. He saw religion as inhibiting change.
- promoted a faith in both natural and social science.
- presented a utopian idealistic view, based on materialistic arguments.

Emile Durkheim presented a functionalist analysis:

- The aim was to discover the sources of social order and stability in order to prevent social breakdown. Its traditions were therefore conservative, to preserve the social systems of societies.
- People in a state of nature were seen as egotistical creatures who could only be controlled by the power of social rules. Society was able to exert such influence so long as people recognised the legitimacy of institutions and shared common goals and values.
- Among the most influential of these was religion, which laid down rules of behaviour and established rituals and provided symbols which gave people a sense of community.

Max Weber:

- insisted that sociology should be concerned with the individual rather than groups or collectives. His starting point was the individual's subjective meanings.
- analysed the relationship between a particular set of religious values (Calvinism) and a particular kind of economic mentality (rational capitalism).
- showed how religion can promote major developments in society, whereas both functionalists and Marxists described the processes by which it is a conservative force, inhibiting change.
- Parkin paraphrases the message in Weber's sociology of religion:

'tell me the position that any class or stratum occupies in the division of labour... and I will tell you the general nature of the religious beliefs to which its members subscribe.'

Parkin (1982)

The ways in which people give meaning to their world and the role which religion plays in this process is taken up and developed by more recent sociologists (especially Peter Berger and Thomas Luckmann) who work in the Weberian tradition, which is discussed in Chapter 4.

STUDY GUIDES

Group work

1   Divide into groups, to represent the views of Marx, Durkheim and Weber. Examine the details relating to the religious practices in Haiti and Venezuela detailed below. Suggest how each theorist would have interpreted the information.

Voodoo is a magical and animistic cult in which groups meet for special magical ceremonies. Trances are induced by spirit possession. Other elements include drum and dance, animal sacrifice and aspects of Roman Catholic liturgy. It is found especially in Haiti, an economically poor country, but religiously very strong. There are large numbers of Catholics, Baptists, Seventh Day Adventists, Mormons and Pentacostalists in the country. Voodoo practices are officially opposed, but they attract large numbers of Haitian peasants. There are estimated to be 15,000 voodooist priests. Many of the greatest military leaders of the country were practitioners. It is also thought to have influenced many leaders of the new independence movement. Ceremonies are often held in secret, last for several hours and involve much singing and dancing. Some of the leading practitioners want the religion to become legitimised and taught in schools. They argued that the power of the religion in the past helped them cast off slavery, and inspired the overthrow of the dictator Duvalier, and it ought now to be accepted.

In Venezuela, the cult of Maria Lionza attracts more than 50,000 people in annual celebrations and is especially popular in poor areas. The faithful believe that spirits can work through mediums to bring prosperity to people for a fee of about £30. It combines local rituals with aspects of Christianity and witchcraft. They involve speaking in tongues, dancing on hot coals and sacrificing animals. The occult is a strong feature of Venezuelan society.

---

2   Discuss the following questions in small groups:
   a   What is meant by the term 'Protestant ethic'? Explain why the Protestant Ethic thesis is important to Weber's analysis of the role of religion in society. Are Protestants more successful than members of other religious groups in modern society?
   b   In which areas of social life does religion influence behaviour? Why is the Conservative Party sometimes described as 'the Church of England at prayer'?
   c   Discuss the following statements and decide whether they are Marxist, Functionalist or Weberian views. Give examples to illustrate the statements.

Religion is:
    A unified system of beliefs and practices relative to sacred things
    An ideological system used by the ruling class to control others
    A series of illusionary myths that obscure and distort reality
    A means of maintaining the norms and mores of the society
    A means of providing people with meaning and structure to their lives
    The product of alienation
    A reflection of the 'collective conscience'
    A source of social change
    A major factor in the development of modern capitalism.

Key Concepts activity

Each group to define and discuss the terms listed on pp 21–22, with examples from their own experience. Write the definition on a Key Concept Card for revision purposes (see p 3).

Practice questions

1 'The main function of religion in society is to promote social solidarity and harmony.' Evaluate sociological arguments and evidence both for and against this statement.
2 Compare and contrast Marxist and Weberian views on the role of religion in society.
3 Assess the evidence for and against the claim that religion is either a conservative force in society or a force for social change.

Coursework suggestions

1 Is there evidence to show that people who practise their religion on a regular basis: are more conservative in terms of their attitudes about monarchy, trade unions, schools, immigration issues and other relevant social matters, than a sample of non-religious people?
2 Establish some major similarities and differences between a sample of religious people who regularly attend a church and a sample of fanatical football fans or members of other associations or organisations.
3 Undertake an observational study of a religious group, service or ceremonies, as if observed by a person from another planet who has no knowledge of what is going on. Examine the role of ritual and ceremony in the lives of people on a day to day basis. What functions do they serve?

4

CONTEMPORARY THEORIES OF RELIGION

Introduction

THIS CHAPTER EXAMINES the more contemporary theories of religion, listed in the table below.

Table 5: *Perspectives, concepts, theorists and ideas in this chapter*			
PERSPECTIVE	KEY CONCEPTS	KEY THEORISTS	KEY IDEAS
Phenomenology	Meaning Social construction Plausibility structure Universe of meaning Nomos Cosmos Theodicy Disenchantment Sacred canopy	Peter Berger Thomas Luckmann	Religion gives meaning to the universe
Neo Marxist	Hegemony Dominant ideology Liberation theology Power elites	Antonio Gramsci Otto Maduro Nicholas Abercrombie Bryan Turner Ralph Milliband	Religion can be a source of revolutionary movements
Neo Functionalist	Ritual Rites of passage Civil religion Consensus	Bronislaw Malinowski Kingsley Davis Talcott Parsons Charles Glock Robert Bellah Thomas O'Dea Guy Swanson	Religion influences cultural systems and provides support for people

Exchange Theory	Costs Rewards Compensation Compensators	Rodney Stark William Bainbridge	Religion provides rewards in exchange for the costs of uncertainty in life
Feminist Theory	Patriarchy Witchcraft Control Subordination	Pamela Abbott Claire Wallace	Religion has been used to control women
Postmodernist	Relativism Privatised religion Choice End of ideology	Jean-Francois Lyotard	Religion is whatever you want it to be

PHENOMENOLOGY

Phenomenology (interactionism or interpretive sociology) is the descriptive study of experiences. Phenomenologists believe that there is an inner subjective, reflective, imaginative world which gives rise to the meanings which people place on the events of the physical world. People interact, observe the behaviour of others, draw conclusions and act upon them. To study the meanings it is necessary to see the world through the eyes of the people involved; this will reveal their interpretations and explain their behaviour. For example, a Christian man in a foreign country who attends a religious service, may act inappropriately because he does not understand the social rules of the religious group. The hostile responses of members of the congregation would be based on their perceptions of his apparent deviancy.

THE SOCIAL CONSTRUCTION OF SOCIETY

Berger explains that society is socially constructed. He means that people build up a knowledge of their everyday world through their experiences and make sense of their environment in their interactions with others. They categorise and classify phenomena and build a common sense knowledge of their society. He says that 'Society is a human product and nothing but a human product, that yet continuously acts back upon its producer'.

Religion is a very significant social institution which categorises the world into the sacred and secular, the moral and the evil. It provides people with a set of beliefs and ethical codes which become part of their subjective understanding, everyday knowledge which helps them to make sense of life – described as 'the universe of meaning'.

The universe of meaning

Berger says that 'all social life is precarious; all societies are constructions in the face of chaos'. This universe of meaning is socially created; it arises from the myths, customs, values and central belief systems of the society. For example, young males may be taught that

---

'one must be brave because one wants to become a real man; one must perform rituals because otherwise the gods will be angry; one must be loyal to the chief because if one does the gods will support one in time of danger...'

The Social Construction of Reality, 1967

This serves to provide stability in the society by supporting it with meanings shared by the majority of its members. (Those who do not, can be usefully identified as deviants or problems, and treated accordingly.)

The support systems which people construct to give meaning to their world are subject to disruption as societies undergo change and development. The evolutionary theories of Darwin in the last 40 years of the nineteenth century undermined the traditional stories from Genesis which had previously been unquestioned as to the origins of the earth and mankind. The ideas which come to be accepted as legitimate are described by Berger and Luckmann as 'a sacred canopy', which stretches over society as a protective cover.

Without this, they argue, the whole universe of meaning would fall apart; life would become meaningless and the stability of society would be threatened. Religion helps to create, sustain and legitimate universes of meaning. Berger says:

Most of what we know we have taken on the authority of others, and it is only as others continue to confirm this knowledge that it continues to be plausible to us. It is this that allows us to move with a measure of confidence through everyday life'.

A Rumour of Angels, 1970

NOMOS, COSMOS AND THEODICY

1 The **nomos** is the orderly world people produce through processes of interaction and observation of others. It helps us become effective citizens. Berger says that 'every nomos is an area of meaning carved out of a vast mass of meaninglessness, a small clearing of lucidity in a formless, dark, always ominous jungle'.
2 The **cosmos** describes the ways in which the influence of religious values makes the whole universe humanly significant. It is the way in which chaos is kept at bay.

3 **Theodicy** is the explanation of the paradox of a just God who allows pain and suffering. People encounter such conflicts when they meet a particular kind of experience, such as bereavement, divorce, imprisonment, or personal hostility of all kinds. Berger sees these as especially dangerous times.

People turn to various forms of help in times of crisis. While science and the arts can help to resolve difficult questions, religion also plays a potentially special role in protecting people from anomie, alienation and despair.

PLAUSIBILITY STRUCTURE

The systems which people build to maintain credible explanations of the world and its mysteries are described by Berger as **plausibility structures**. There is a danger that people can become detached from religious convictions and the protections they afford if this plausibility structure is undermined. For example, new philosophical interpretations may attack traditional views (see p 97).

To reassert their power to shape social thought, opportunities are taken to legitimate and infuse major social dramas with special religious rituals and rites; eg in Britain, monarchs are crowned in a Cathedral by an Archbishop. This is part of the protective canopy of legitimation.

RATIONALISATION AND DISENCHANTMENT

When people are faced with competing belief systems and alternative ways of living, their lives are subject to a process of dissonance and periods of crisis. Where there are no certainties, there is the possibility of meaninglessness, disorder and anomie. Weber had pointed out that while the western world was increasingly rational in organisation, relationships became more impersonal. There was a move from Gemeinschaft (community) to Gesellschaft (association) and a process of religious demystification, accompanied by the growth of **disenchantment**. Berger describes how these dangers have been intensified with the growth of modern technologies and media, which increase choices and make the world a more fragmented place. Religion loses its traditional appeals and people become 'homeless', deprived of all those supports which they used to have. There are few certainties or absolutes; it is hard to decide the moral way to behave in a situation, because there can be no absolute agreement as to the answer.

It is phenomenologists' hope that modern society will rediscover the supernatural and reestablish the structures that give meaning to life. If the protective canopy is shattered or the plausibility beliefs undermined, then the whole universe of meaning can be destroyed.

- Religion is important to society because it is a source of legitimacy. Laws are legitimised by sacred commandments. For example, 'thou shalt not kill'; marriage is defined as holy matrimony. Parliamentary business cannot begin until prayers are said.
- It links meaning with ultimate reality.
- It presents a humanising presence in a society, and makes sense of a person's place in the universe. Berger describes it as 'one of the most effective bulwarks against anomie throughout human history'.
- It operates with concepts of the divine and the supernatural, and takes account of the entire cosmos; it carries great authority.

Study point

Do you agree with Berger's view that religion has been one of the most effective bulwarks against anomie throughout human history? Has it helped people develop a greater sense of involvement in their community? Consider factors such as age, gender, ethnicity.

EVALUATION

Strengths

1 Berger provides a useful synthesis of the ideas of Durkheim's functionalism, insights from Marx about the powerful effects that religion can have on the perceptions of people about the world, and Weber's emphasis on the significance of the meaning of events and systems on behaviour.
2 The view provides a strong justification for the retention of religious rites and ceremonies in schools and in wider society, to sustain the plausibility structures without which many people may develop a sense of anomie and detachment from society.

Points of criticism

1 Berger and Luckmann assume (like functionalists) that religion provides only positive functions in society such as promoting social stability and order. They overlook the ways in which religion can encourage and promote social conflict.
2 They fail to consider the possible significance of functional alternatives to orthodox religious theologies, which may provide a great deal of support, integration and community identity.
3 They do not consider the examples of societies in which religion does not appear to be very significant (eg, in China) or where it is a possible source of social division, yet the society does not necessarily collapse in disorder.

4 They make use of mystical notions, like nomos and cosmos, which are not open to analysis.

Activity

Write short definitions of the following terms on a large sheet of paper and show the interconnections between each of them:

- Interaction
- Social meaning
- Cosmos
- Theodicy
- Phenomenology

- Legitimate
- Nomos
- Norms
- Social construction of reality

NEO-MARXISM

Writers who have subsequently adopted and adapted the ideas of Marx are known as neo-Marxists. Some have examined the ways in which religion can serve to resist the power of ruling elites, rather than seeing it as a tool of oppression.

Antonio Gramsci used the term **hegemony** to describe the process whereby a powerful group exercises control over the consciousness, beliefs and values of another section of society. He argues that those who defend the interests of working class people would themselves need to establish a popular hegemonic ideology, which would enable that of the ruling elite to be undermined. He also argues that religion could be an agency of resistance to attacks on a society or state; in this respect it becomes a potential source of change, rather than necessarily upholding the status quo. Widely held religious principles could therefore become a valuable force for liberation. Milliband has drawn on Gramsci's concept of hegemony to argue that there is, in western capitalist societies,

---

'a process of massive indoctrination conducted through a multitude of agencies, to dissuade members of the subordinate classes to hold or express unorthodox views...'

Otto Maduro also developed some of Gramsci's ideas and argued that the defenders of the working class position could be concerned members of the priesthood. They could politicise the working class and develop practical **liberation theologies**. Such approaches have developed a radical interpretation of the effects of Christianity in certain economic and political situations, examining the ways that Christianity has been concerned with the sufferings of people. The ideas of Marx have been used to analyse the nature of the injustices that exist, and then to mobilise the teaching of Christianity to show how people can liberate themselves from the problems that confront them.

Such movements have occurred in parts of South America, where concern about poverty and the exploitation of resources by foreign powers and local dictators were voiced by Catholic priests. They also sought to ensure that poor people recognised the issues and acted effectively. In some cases these priest-revolutionaries were killed by government forces, which heightened the levels of awareness of problems and resulted in further violent reaction.

Nicholas Abercrombie and **Bryan Turner** (1978) examined the Marxist thesis that in most societies, there is a set of beliefs which dominate all others and which tend to inhibit the development of radical political dissent through their effects on the consciousness of subordinate classes. In Britain, the beliefs would include acceptance of the status quo, in which the rich and powerful are to be admired and deserve deference. These theorists question the view that religion is a source of ideological control. Their claims:

- The subordinate classes are not incorporated into this **dominant ideology**.
- Traditionally the peasantry were separated from the official mysteries of the church by language (Latin) and mystical rituals. The teachings of the church were therefore likely to be largely impenetrable to the subordinate classes.
- Even the clergy were an unreliable channel for orthodox Christian belief. Many were too badly educated to provide sermons.
- In Victorian Britain the two main classes were two races apart with different religions, moralities and politics:

Primary and secondary evidence points to the fact that in terms of religion and morality, the working class and the capitalist class occupied separate cultures.

The Dominant Ideology Thesis, BJS vol 29 no. 2

They conclude that the real significance of religion for the power elites was an attempt to guarantee the **family** as a mechanism for the conservation of property, functioning to provide a degree of normative coherence in the dominant class. They accept that this has changed in recent times as great wealth is also held by powerful organisations and companies; the family structure is changing also, with increasing rates of divorce and illegitimacy.

Study point

Consider this Jesuitical view (a Catholic teaching order): 'give me the child at the age of seven and I will give you the man'.

Activity

1 Discuss some of the ways that sociologists could investigate the following issues:
   a There is/is not a dominant ideology, justifying the wealth and power of the very rich and powerful, which is widely accepted.
   b Religion is increasingly less important in sustaining it.
2 Discuss some of the problems that would arise in undertaking such research.

NEO-FUNCTIONALISM

Writers who have made use of the insights of Durkheim and introduced additional ideas to his Functionalist theories are known as neo-functionalists.

Bronislaw Malinowski, an anthropologist, also emphasised the very positive functions of religion, when he suggested that religion offers people ways in which they can manage their tensions and reduce their anxieties during times of social disruption and crisis. He said religion provides 'the comforting view, the culturally valuable belief in immortality … in the ceremonies at death … religion gives body and form to the saving beliefs…'. He considers it socially dangerous to have people unable to function effectively if faced by anxiety or other severe emotional disability.

Kingsley Davis echoes this positive view of religion when he said 'the existence of goals beyond this world serve to compensate people for the frustrations they inevitably experience in striving to reach socially valuable ends. It replaces possibly dangerous aggression with a faith in the unseen …'. He argued that by providing individuals with an understanding of a world beyond this one, they are able to interpret any crisis or disaster in ways that leave them able to continue their lives in effective and purposeful ways.

Talcott Parsons considered that the problem of social order was a central concern for sociologists. Religion socialised people into acceptable ways of acting; patterns of norms developed within a culture, which provided the basis of unity and social harmony. In western society, for example, many of these guidelines emerge from the Ten Commandments.

This function gives religion a social value. In addition, it helps to provide stability in society by providing opportunities for national unity (in times of national crisis or loss); it imposes meaning on apparently meaningless events ('it is part of God's plan'; 'it is a test of moral character').

Charles Glock and **Robert Bellah** undertook research into new religious movements which emerged in USA in the 1960s, explaining these as a rejection of the traditional values of utilitarian individualism. They suggested there was a new religious consciousness emerging, and many of the Civil Rights leaders were ordained ministers and priests. This shows a commitment to a more egalitarian America, in which there is greater sense of community. The decline in institutional religion and a move towards more individualistic interpretations is part of the movement towards a *civil* religion, in which there is both faith in God and in America.

- Their work follows the views of Durkheim that traditional forms of religion cannot survive in a modern world, but new secular or civil ones will emerge to replace them or fulfil the functions of the original ones. An executive of the McDonald's chain said 'I speak of faith in McDonalds as if it were a religion. I believe in God, family and McDonalds...' (quoted in *The McDonaldisation of Society*, Ritzger, 1995).
- Religion is made up of belief systems which help to integrate and bind society into a unified whole, a moral community. On this view, the massive popular response of the public to the death of Diana, Princess of Wales in 1997, in which hundreds of thousands of people massed around Buckingham Palace, signed books of remembrance and shared in the funeral ceremonies, had a spiritual element. Only a small proportion of those people were regular churchgoers, yet they were involved in a spontaneous civil religious activity, in which they were expressing spiritual needs and concerns.

Thomas O'Dea argues that religion operates with ideas and concepts which are beyond the physical world, but which are concerned with its unpredictabilities. People require stability when faced with frustrations and difficulties. This need leads them towards religious explanations, which promote community goals and values. Life's setbacks become relatively unimportant when there is a long-term goal to be achieved. The functions of religion are to provide:

- support in crisis; a stable society which is legitimised
- teachers of ethics and an awareness of the common good
- a source of identity
- valuable opportunities to indulge in **rites of passage**, especially those of birth, marriage and death, which instil social unity.

At the same time he recognises that it may provide such strong sense of identity that it causes friction with other religious groups.

POINTS OF EVALUATION

1 Studies of conformity (Asch, 1956) show that people like to be part of a majority and a community who share things in common. It is uncomfortable to be an outsider.
2 O'Dea emphasises the ways that religion integrates people and unites them, especially in times of difficulty. He also recognises how in the past functionalists have undervalued possible dysfunctional effects of religion and the ways in which it can promote change.

Activity
List six points to show how Neo-functionalists, such as O'Dea, would interpret the events surrounding the death and funeral of Diana, Princess of Wales, in August 1997.

Guy Swanson examines Durkheim's argument that when worshipping in religious ceremonies, people are in fact venerating society itself. He put it to an empirical test by analysing comparative data from 50 societies to establish their modes of religious organisation and patterns of beliefs. He wished to see whether it was true that if religion emerged from the experiences of social life, then variations in cultural experiences within societies would explain the different patterns of practice and belief, including the different characteristics of their deities and spirits.

He analysed statistical evidence and found that the more hierarchically structured societies with clear status distinctions, were associated with such features as belief in an omnipotent creator and polytheism. Those which made use of a highly significant kinship structure, practised ancestor worship; whereas reincarnation was predominant in societies in which individuals had high status in localised areas. Witchcraft practices were found where there were few legitimated social controls on activities (woman practicing medicine in times and places where it was a male preserve). The data seemed to support the view that religion declines in societies where people take more control of their own destinies.

Hamilton criticises Swanson's work because:

- he does not examine a fundamental issue – why there should necessarily be a symbolic explanation of social structures in simple societies which takes a religious form. Why should it be necessary to invest a bull-roarer with magical powers or create totems?
- he relies too much on his statistical data to support his conclusions, for which there could be other interpretations.

EXCHANGE THEORY

Rodney Stark and **William Bainbridge** developed an analysis which had its basis in psychological theories of **reward** and **cost**, known as exchange theory. This had been taken up by sociologist **George Homans,** who examined the ways in which exchange (mutual help, advice and other socially valued acts) was central to the maintenance of stable relationships between people. Exchange theory suggests that people are never altruistic in their actions. Everything is done for reward, and some acts are avoided because they are too costly.

Study point
How would exchange theory explain a person risking their life by jumping in a river to save someone?

OUTLINE OF STARK AND BAINBRIDGE'S EXCHANGE THEORY:

- Religion serves to provide answers and **compensations**, to people seeking information about how to achieve the goals, where they cannot be certain of attaining them.
- The **compensators** are explanations which stand in the place of the actual rewards and are accepted as a matter of faith because they are so strongly wanted and so hard to achieve.
- By offering people compensators, they are encouraged to act in ways which will bring them the promised rewards and outweigh any costs. In this way the compensators meet the spiritual needs of people.
- People turn to deities when they cannot satisfy their needs for understanding or other of their desires remain unfulfilled. They offer a supernaturally based set of explanations and help resolve feelings of discontent.
- Although the organisations which inform people about such things may fade and disappear, as membership dwindles or becomes attached to another group, religion itself cannot disappear because it is the source of the supernatural compensating explanations for every new generation.

POINTS OF EVALUATION

1   Stark and Bainbridge present a theory which shares some things in common with functionalist explanations – it is one of the functions of religion to provide general compensations to enable people to retain a sense of optimism about the future.

2 They share some things in common with phenomenologists – religion provides meanings for people through supernatural explanations (a kind of plausibility structure).

3 They make assertions which may be hard to justify – why should humans assume that the source of desired rewards are with deities?

4 Not everyone would agree that belief in an after-life is a compensation for death. The idea of an endless heaven or hell may be unacceptable to some.

5 The term compensator has a negative implication, an inferior substitute for what people want but are unable to obtain.

6 Their theory helps to explain why churches which move away from a stress on the supernatural lose membership, as they are disregarding human needs and failing to supply the reward support system. Evangelical and other ethnic religious groups are attracting membership. These do place emphasis on the supernatural, the emotional and the idea of direct contact with a deity.

FEMINIST THEORY

Pamela Abbott and Claire Wallace identify seven different feminist perspectives: liberal/reformist, Marxist, radical, dual-systems, postmodernist, materialist and black feminist. All address the same question of what constitutes the oppression of women, and all suggest strategies for overcoming it. They argue that because it is the aim of sociology to understand the social world and the roles of people in it, feminist theory has been concerned with enabling women (and men) to understand the subordination and exploitation of women. Unless the criticisms of feminists are taken into account, sociology will continue to produce distorted accounts of the social world and women's position in it.

From this shared perspective, it can be argued that because the male has traditionally been seen to be the most powerful and dominant of the sexes, religious belief has a basis in **patriarchal ideology**.

- All religious movements are male centred, through teachers and prophets. The church service illustrates how deep-rooted the masculine nature of the church is, using male pronouns and commands for women to take a subservient role. 'Let the women learn in silence with all subjection' (1 Tim, 2.11); 'All wickedness is but little to the wickedness of a woman' (Ecc, 25.19); 'He is in the glory of the God; but woman is the glory of the man' (1 Cor, 14.35).

- Religious organisations have emerged which have tended to legitimate gender inequalities both through their power holders and beliefs they develop, in which women invariably play a subsidiary role.

- Some church leaders have recently claimed that women are incapable of taking leadership roles, claiming that biologically, men take the initiative.

RELIGION AS A SOURCE OF CONTROL

Family life

Religious institutions advocate traditional family structures. This helps to place women in a more subservient role as carers and home makers, servicing the family members at the expense of their own careers and opportunities. In this respect religion acts as an agency of **social control** of women and children. The Koran says 'Men are in charge of women ... hence good women are obedient'. In the Bible, Ephesians 5, 22–24 says 'wives, be subject to your husbands ... for the husband is the head of the wife ...'. In Judaism, there is a prayer in which males say 'Blessed art thou, O Lord ... that I was not born a woman'.

Property ownership

Religious beliefs serve to legitimate male ownership of property and the inheritance through a male line or to those children who are decreed to be legitimate. (It is only in comparatively recent times that women, cohabiting on a permanent unmarried basis, have gained the right to an equal share in property if the relationship breaks down.)

Activity

Read the following account and explain why this evangelical group is criticised by radical feminists and by those who see it as a right wing political movement, whereas other women support its aims. Which group do you think is right?

In 1996, over a million men attended rallies in USA organised by The Promise Keepers, founded in 1990 and said to be America's fastest growing religious group. Its revenues already exceed $96m. An estimated 750,000 met in Washington in 1997. Their message is 'Real men Love Jesus'. T-shirts and baseball caps proclaim 'Real men Sing Real Loud'; 'Proud to be a Dad'. There are books and videos on sale with titles like 'How to Dad'. There are experts on hand to advise on 'Christian Financial Concepts' and 'The Biblical Way of Managing Money' and ministries for the 'Relationally and Sexually Broken'. Many famous sportsmen offer their support; golfers like Paul Azinger and Bernhard Langer invite golfing members of the Keepers to 'use their golf for the glory of God'. The Promise Keepers, with branches in Britain, is an exclusively male group, committed to honouring Jesus through worship, prayer and obedience to God's word; understanding that they need brothers to help them keep their promises; practising spiritual and sexual purity; building strong marriages and families, in which they take full responsibility and control; supporting the mission of their religious organisation; reaching beyond racial and denominational barriers to demonstrate the power of biblical unity. The wife of the founder, a football coach, complained that for a year he was unaware of her bulimia and suicidal depression 'and never fixed anything in the home'.

Adapted from articles in The Independent, 1996, The Guardian, 1997 and The Observer, 1997

Witchcraft

Witches were invariably identified as being feminine, evil and anti-Christ.

Power (1975) has said

'The view of women as an instrument of the devil, a thing at once inferior and evil, took shape in the earliest period of Church history and was indeed originated by the church.'

Medieval Woman, 1975

In the period 1300–1500 it has been established that two-thirds of all those defined as witches were women. The trend continued into the sixteenth and seventeenth centuries. It is now an assumption taken for granted in any child's book of fairy stories.

Smout (1973) has estimated that in Scotland between 1560–1707, more than 3,000 people perished as witches. As the legal and social status of women improved, together with the development of a more rational and scientific based society, there was a decline in the number of witch persecutions.

Simone de Beauvoir said

'In the sixteenth century all European legal codes were erected on a basis of canon law (religious law), Roman law and Germanic law – all unfavourable to women.'

The Second Sex, 1972

There was a clear linking of the social inferiority of women with their spiritual inferiority among both Catholic and Protestant theologians (including Luther and Calvin).

Abbott and **Wallace** quote research which suggests that there is a link between the campaign to suppress female healing work and the attack on women as witches. Women were subjected to claims of witchcraft because as carers and mothers they were more familiar with remedies for ill health than men and so they were traditionally more likely to take on the role of village healers. This came to be a source of friction as men took exception to this work. (In Britain it was not until 1899 that an Act of Parliament removed all legal barriers to women training as doctors.)

Sexuality and the body

Michel Foucault has argued that power is prominent in every aspect of our lives, because it involves thought and knowledge which is accepted in the culture. Religion plays a role in this process of verification. He has drawn attention to the ways in which social institutions (such as religion, education and penal institutions) can exert power by controlling the human body. They influence relationships and the ways in which we think and act. Religious values within different cultures may control all kinds of activities in relation to the body. These include:

- dietary arrangements, the time people eat, and what they may or may not eat. Most religions encourage times of fasting and abstinence.
- dress: some religions prescribe a veil (or hijab) for women; older Catholic women still tend to cover their head in church (whereas men must not).
- religious rules which influence other bodily functions, relating to family arrangements, such as rules of consummating a marriage, the bearing of children and abortion.

ISLAM

Charlotte Butler (1995) illustrates the power of religion to shape patterns of thought and behaviour, and showed that for second generation Muslim women in Britain, Islam continues to represent the major guide to life with which they construct their individual identities and lifestyles. However, there are those who argue that the rules regarding dress are not controlling, but rather liberating. For some, adherence to Islam and its codes enables women to construct roles that give them more freedom and choice; there could be advantages in wearing the traditional dress which doesn't draw the attention of males to the female body (the norm in a western society), providing greater levels of security in a sexist society.

THE CHURCH OF ENGLAND

Although the first community of deaconesses in the Church of England was established in 1860, and a decision was passed in 1975 to allow the ordination of women as priests by the Church Synod, it was not until March 1994 that the first 32 women priests were finally ordained. (A movement for Catholic Women's Ordination is hoping to achieve similar success.) The result has been that between 500–1000 male clergy have left the Anglican Church in protest. Feminists argue that there is no biblical demand that the priesthood should be of one gender. Their number now exceeds 1500. The attempt to use legal means to ban the ordination of women was finally closed in 1997 when a clergyman was prevented from continuing his campaign, because he was wasting the court's time and money. An analysis of the Scriptures was made by Elizabeth Stanton in 1895 entitled *The Women's Bible*, which argued that the equality intended between the sexes by God was not reflected in the Bible, because it had been written by men.

THE CATHOLIC CHURCH

Andrew Brown notes how feminists in the early 1990s managed to delay a translation of a Catholic catechism for two years by arguing for changes to the language used which was considered by them to be too male-orientated. The major concession they obtained was the introduction of female altar servers.

The work of feminists in attacking traditional doctrine has been effective in raising the consciousness of Catholic women (and some men) so that the Church has become more tolerant of the use of artificial methods of birth control. Brown notes how in this area 'the Vatican has stopped struggling against democracy and started to struggle against feminism instead'. However, he is optimistic that resistance to democracy will crumble in due course since women have much to offer and have important roles to play. Interestingly, in 1997, 2.3 million Catholics endorsed a five-point declaration in favour of ordaining women priests, and changing the teachings with regard to contraception.

THE FEMALE IMAGE IN RELIGION

- Female deities are found in all religions throughout the world. In some they take on a motherly caring role (as in Christianity, with Mary, the Mother of God) and in others they appear as threatening and dangerous. There seem to be few in which they are dominant icons, because of the predominance of male power.
- In the Christian religion, women who entered religious orders played their role of carers as nuns, who may have assisted priests in the preparation of sacred sacraments for mass; and worked as teachers or nurses.
- Catholic feminists argue that the Catholic Church has allowed Mary to epitomise women's roles, leading a life in submission to God and an unhelpful role model to young girls. They would like to see her recognised as a co-redeemer. Father Tissa Balasuriya sees her as an early political activist promoting the views of her revolutionary son after his death.

WOMEN AND RELIGIOUS INVOLVEMENT

Statistics show that women display more qualities of religious behaviour than men.

1 Over 60 per cent of regular and frequent church attenders are women. From a conflict perspective women are an exploited group: in Britain they have traditionally suffered more disadvantages than men; they are paid less; they tend to have lower status (the majority are working in service industries and few reach top positions of power). Therefore, they make more use of religion as a form of consolation.

2 A higher proportion of women are active in smaller sects and denominations. This may be because they offer more opportunities to women to be accepted and to use their range of skills appropriately. They provide an opportunity for status advancement which the mainstream churches do not.

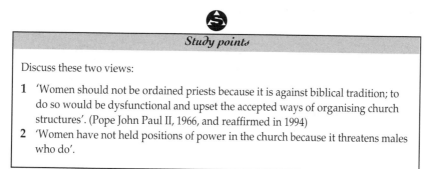

Study points

Discuss these two views:

1 'Women should not be ordained priests because it is against biblical tradition; to do so would be dysfunctional and upset the accepted ways of organising church structures'. (Pope John Paul II, 1966, and reaffirmed in 1994)
2 'Women have not held positions of power in the church because it threatens males who do'.

POSTMODERNISM

Postmodernists argue that the attempt to apply scientific procedures to obtain what is assumed to be an objective truth about a society, is a mistaken one. They claim that:

- societies are dynamic and fluid and constantly changing
- there are only relative values
- all the old beliefs in absolute truths have been lost. There is an end of ideologies.

In Britain, political parties no longer hold traditional ideological values which were once sacrosanct, recognising that they no longer have meaning for a majority of voters. The churches are accused of altering their doctrines according to the direction of the moral winds of change. The French philosopher, **Lyotard**, writing in 1984, said that there has been a demise of the belief in scientific rationality as a source of positive truth about the world, and a return of multiple wisdoms, cultures and a relativism of knowledge. There can be no belief in progress, since it is neither feasible nor desirable.

Postmodern society has many characteristics. One is that people in a fractured society gain a sense of their identity as a result of their selection of lifestyle, social and leisure activities from the cultural alternatives provided in a pluralist, multi-cultural society. Another, is that people (including sociologists) are inevitably subject to the processes of **relativism**.

- They must come to terms with the loss of certainties and absolute values which define morality. There can be no universal truths (whether scientific or religious). There are many different ways of understanding and interpreting events, ideas and beliefs.

- New ideas and information are constantly impinging on people's awareness of the world. It is possible to believe in aspects of any number of competing ideologies without belonging to any one group from which they emerge. It is no longer easy to define the distinctions between faiths in order to state clearly the one to which one 'belongs'.
- Religion becomes more personal, a 'privatised' matter; people may find themselves selecting from those parts of belief systems which they favour most and shape them into personal philosophies. In the past, a religious group provided clear messages and provided an identity for an individual which was not open to negotiation.
- The nature of faith is becoming relative to time and place, and its range and scope is open to change to suit the changing needs of people in contemporary society at the end of the twentieth century.

There are many consequences of this analysis. It implies a collapse in religious belief systems, in political ideologies and the emergence of a new kind of society.

POINTS OF EVALUATION

Such views make Weber's idea that to know a person's class and status is to know their religious values, increasingly less likely; according to the postmodernist view, all these factors are changing in a fluid way. By the same token, Durkheim's view that shared religious rituals, beliefs and values acts as a social cement, holding a society together, is also undermined.

Habermas is a critic of the postmodern analysis. He argues that it represents a dangerously conservative attack on the Enlightenment project; ie, the development of rational, scientific methods, which have not yet been fully worked out, but which will eventually be successful.

John Eldridge of the Glasgow Media Group has argued that it is a mistaken view to think that it is a pointless task to build knowledge about the world through gathering evidence which can be subjected to critical analysis. This is the task of sociology and other social sciences. The postmodernist abandonment of this project is described by him as 'intellectual vertigo … a failure of nerve'.

Madeleine Bunting describes how religious belief is becoming a DIY cocktail. She notes that:

- 70 per cent profess a belief in God; 10–15 per cent attend regularly; 30 per cent are seasonal attenders (Christmas or Easter).
- People are dipping into different beliefs and taking from them what appeals most, and then reject them later if they become redundant. The mainstream orthodox churches have made some attempts to respond by updating services and introducing aspects to appeal to younger people; one offers 'a funky

mellow worship and dance'. In the search for spiritual experience, the aim is to provide people with better ways of living and an internal spiritual balance.

'Vestiges of Christianity such as carols and cribs now jostle alongside neo-paganism, astrology, tarot cards, palmistry, self help New Age therapies and Transcendental Meditation'.

The Guardian, 1996

- A Church of England Report in 1996, *Search for Faith*, stated that Britain is operating a spiritual free market. There is a dangerous fragmentation of beliefs and the loss of clear boundaries between different faiths.
- In Japan there is a similar model. People use Shinto, Buddhism or Christianity as they see fit. The result is that numerous new religions emerge mixing aspects of the different traditions. In Britain, many eminent people appear to be adopting similar approaches in their private lives.
- Members of the Royal Family are indulging in New Age therapies as well as consulting astrologers, healers and therapists.
- Popular magazines devote pages to 'psychic chic', especially Feng-shui, a Chinese belief in the power of furniture arrangement to promote health. Even high street stores have shown an interest. On television, Mystic Meg is currently a national figure, as are various astrologers advising people watching mass audience chat shows.
- Various programmes dealing with the paranormal have become popular, and reading the daily horoscope is increasingly acceptable. People are turning away from traditional religions and seeking advice and help from healers, psychics and clairvoyants.
- Some have argued that this movement represents the future of religion. It is more about the quality of the experience than belief or the truth of the doctrine. The rave culture of the 1990s places a similar emphasis on experience outside the normal, which perhaps accounts for their use of drug ecstacy.

Management courses offer training which incorporates New Age self-help therapies, as an aid to operating effectively in the world of big business. This, like everyone else's daily life, is precarious. People are therefore seeking clues as to what the future might hold, and this is the basis of the existence of a range of sects, many of which offer bizarre belief systems to members (such as those which led to disasters at Waco and to the followers of the Order of the Solar Temple).

In their analysis of the attractions of such movements, commentators have looked at the ways in which young people are attracted to the opportunities to pick and mix:

- For some, it is because they are always keen to try new experiences.
- Others have considered the fact that there is a loss in belief in science as the force of human progress; the values of socialism and communism appear to

have failed; the Thatcherite revolution of the enterprise culture has not developed; there is no sense of optimism about the future. The new spiritual movements from which people can select work on a more personal level.

- Paul Heelas suggests that there is nothing to fear from the spiritual supermarket; other religious leaders believe that it may mark the decline and fall of orthodox traditional religious organisations. Such loss would also be accompanied by a disappearance of a common moral framework. There is nothing of value to be passed on to subsequent generations in these movements and they offer nothing to hold societies together in the future.

Study point

Postmodernists argue that we cannot distinguish between what is good and bad in cultural life; everything is relative and a matter of taste. Discuss how a religious person might argue that there are absolute values which define right and wrong, moral and immoral behaviour.

STUDY GUIDES

Group work

Can investigations into religion be 'value free'?

Weber said that sociology *should* be 'value free'; researchers should separate their own moral or social beliefs from the project under investigation. Discuss the following issues in small groups.

1 *In analysing religion, sociologists cannot be objective*

Sociologists are members of society and must therefore be influenced by the same factors as those they study. Does the religious background of the sociologist inevitably influence the research and the findings?

2 *In analysing religion they can be objective*

Gouldner has argued that sociologists should always be honest about their personal beliefs (in the way that Berger and Luckmann are). Only in the attempt to gain objectivity will researchers gain intellectual respectability.

3 *Everything is a matter of taste, including religious involvement*

Postmodernists see the idea of a value free scientific approach as a mistaken one. How useful is the DIY image a helpful one in understanding religion today?

Key Concepts activity

Each group to define and discuss the terms listed on pp 41–42, with examples from their own experience. Write the definition on a Key Concept card for revision purposes (see p 3).

Practice questions

1 Neo-functionalists have argued that religion remains important in society because it is a part of the cultural system in society and so supports its central value system. Explain and evaluate this statement.

2 In contemporary Britain, religion competes with leisure pursuits, supermarkets and the mass media for commitment and time. There is evidence to show that religion is unable to attract sufficient support and has less meaning for people than in the past. Critically discuss this view.

3 Neo-Marxists and Weberians argue that religion has a role in the processes of social change in society. Examine and evaluate this approach.

Coursework Suggestions

1 Read Paul Manning's statement below. Is there evidence for this view?

(Note that he also adds that postmodernists are sceptical of all methods which claim to provide knowledge of an ultimate or objective reality. Consider this point in developing your methodology.)

'Postmodernist views would imply that A level sociology students ought to be a fairly jaded and cynical group, disillusioned with all notions of human progress, relativist in their understanding of religion and morality, terminally cynical about policies and political belief systems'.

(Social Science Teacher, vol 25, no.2)

2 Neo-functionalists have argued that religion, rituals and ceremonies help people in societies to feel a stronger sense of community. Do you think that there is evidence to show that school assemblies, major events like a state funeral or coronation serve this function?

3 How widespread are New Age beliefs in your area? Are there high or low levels of knowledge and concern about such movements among the following?
   a local clergy
   b teachers
   c parents
   d young people

SUMMARY

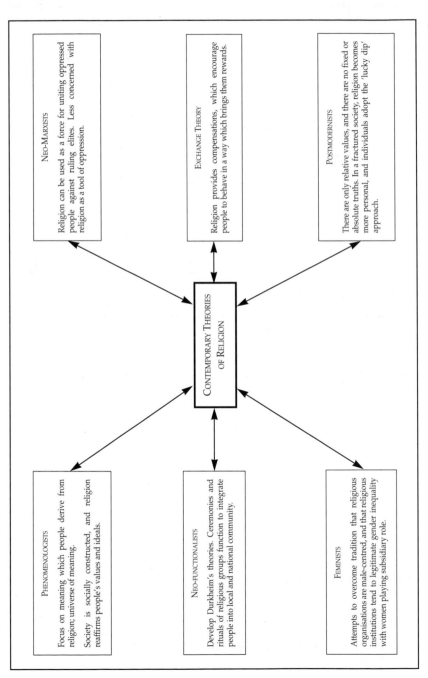

CONTEMPORARY THEORIES OF RELIGION

NEO-MARXISTS

Religion can be used as a force for uniting oppressed people against ruling elites. Less concerned with religion as a tool of oppression.

EXCHANGE THEORY

Religion provides compensations, which encourage people to behave in a way which brings them rewards.

POSTMODERNISTS

There are only relative values, and there are no fixed or absolute truths. In a fractured society, religion becomes more personal, and individuals adopt the 'lucky dip' approach.

PHENOMENOLOGISTS

Focus on meaning which people derive from religion; universe of meaning.

Society is socially constructed, and religion reaffirms people's values and ideals.

NEO-FUNCTIONALISTS

Develop Durkheim's theories. Ceremonies and rituals of religious groups function to integrate people into local and national community.

FEMINISTS

Attempts to overcome tradition that religious organisations are male-centred, and that religious institutions tend to legitimate gender inequality with women playing subsidiary role.

5

RELIGIOUS ORGANISATIONS

Introduction

THIS CHAPTER LOOKS at different types of religious organisations, their attractions for and influence on people and society. It also explores the similarities and differences between them.

Table 6: *Theorists, concepts and issues in this chapter*		
KEY THEORISTS	KEY CONCEPTS	KEY ISSUES
Max Weber	Typologies	• Differences between church denomination, sect and cult
Richard Niebuhr	Church	
Ernst Troeltsch	Denomination Sect	• The significance and analysis of new religious movements
Richard Stark	Cult	
Bryan Wilson	Millenarian Millennial Movements	
Roy Wallis	New Religious Movements	• The significance of Millenarian Movements
Gracie Davie	New Age Movements	

TYPES OF RELIGIOUS ORGANISATION

To make an analysis of social organisations, some sociologists have developed **typologies**. Max Weber and religious historian Ernst Troeltsch advocated a method by which the key features of a social institution are identified so that other organisations can be compared and contrasted. Initially, distinctions were made between a church and a sect. Later, sociologists developed refinements to include analysis of denominations and cults.

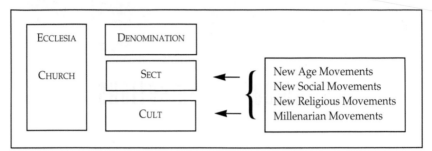

TYPES OF RELIGIOUS ORGANISATION

THE ECCLESIA AND THE CHURCH

ECCLESIA

These are the universal or all-encompassing churches that are allied with the State. They are the largest, most formalised and powerful types of religious organisation. As official religions, Ecclesia are likely to claim all people in a society as members. Often (but not always) there is little tolerance of religious differences within the population. The majority of people of the society may belong to the religion in name only. Examples include the Church of England, the Russian Orthodox Church and Islam in Iran.

THE CHURCH AND THE DENOMINATION

The features of **churches** and **denominations** can be compared and contrasted. The process of establishing a typology of religious organisations has been a fruitful one in sociology. Richard Neibuhr adopted Weber's method and described the denomination in his work in the 1920s, as being between large scale church organisations and small scale groups known as sects. The distinctions in table 7 relate primarily to churches and denominations in British society.

	CHURCH	DENOMINATION
Table 7: *Distinctions between churches and denominations*		
Structure	Large, well established organisation Bureaucratic; priests; vicars and complex hierarchy of paid officials; all have defined authority. Examples: Greek Orthodox Roman Catholic; Anglican (headed by the ruling monarch)	Organisation is smaller than a church Less bureaucratic; ministers and pastors Use of Lay (non ordained) preachers Places of worship: often small chapels Examples: Baptists; Methodists (headed by Conference)
Relations with wider society	Well integrated into social structure Beliefs tend to be conservative and support existing institutions	No formal association with the state Leaders may attend state functions Membership is nationwide
Beliefs and services	Strong use of ritual; no emphasis on emotional response in congregation. Assumption that they hold a monopoly of religious truths. These are explained by professional theologians. More middle class members; (more support for Conservative Party)	Less emphasis on rituals; but emotional fervour through powerful preachers and hymns. Emphasis: personal values May promote special views on alcohol use; books and films; and relate faith to political action. (More support for Lib/Lab parties)
Membership	Inclusive; everyone is offered access to the truths they hold. Conversion is encouraged. Membership at birth through baptism and christening	Not necessarily by birth. No test of merit for members. All are usually accepted who wish to join
Values	Frequently represent the established values of society; close links with sources of political power Monarch head of C of E and the State. Representatives always attend major state functions (coronations; opening of Parliament. Example of a Church opposing central Government: the Catholic Church in Poland (1980s)	No claim to hold universal truths; acceptance that there are many versions of "the truth". Emphasis: A good life. Strong ecumenical values Becker described a denomination as "a sect that has cooled down."
Power	May oppose strongly those who attack or undermine its beliefs and truths. Expulsion possible but unusual. But, people may be barred from its sacraments (example of hierocratic power). This can be an important source of control. Also, Church can exert influence over political leaders and even the monarch. In 1997 the Archbishop of Canterbury spoke effectively to TUC. Also, its hierarchy has seats in the House of Lords.	Limited control over members; there is less emphasis on sacraments so no effective hierocratic power. Less influence in sphere of political and state power

Attractions	They are traditional institutions. There are few demands on members, who are encouraged to be active in the community (not ascetic). The doctrines have historical veracity sustained by expert theologians. Places of worship are often significant buildings. Membership gives a sense of identity and a moral code.	Appeal is to those dissatisfied with mainstream churches or other alternatives. They provide more specific rules for living a good life They may also be more radical than a church without departing too far from a basic conservatism.

Data from Church of England attendance figures on a particular Sunday in the year, provides a figure of 1.8m in 1990. Numbers who may be members at birth would be much higher. There has been a decline in the number of clergy from 20.9 million in 1900 to less than 10 million in 1995.

Table 8: *Attendance (%) by gender and class (Britain) 1991*				
ATTENDANCE	MEN	WOMEN	NON-MANUAL	MANUAL
Frequent	37	63	16	12
Regular	35	65	29	24
Rare/never	48	52	51	61
No response			4	3

SOURCE: BRITISH SOCIAL ATTITUDE SURVEY 1991

Activity

Examine table 8 and suggest some reasons why women appear to be much more religious than men, and why manual workers are less religious than non-manual workers.

Neibuhr suggested that denominations develop from sects which increase in membership over time, become more widely accepted, and are seen to offer something different from the mainstream churches. As they gain wider social respectability, they take on the qualities of a denomination.

Example of a denomination – Methodism
This denomination developed from a Protestant sect, and dates from about 1739 when Anglican priests, John and Charles Wesley began preaching throughout the country. They were barred from Anglican churches, marginalised and

obliged to set up their own organisation. In doing so, Michael Hill suggests they filled a social and ideological vacuum. The effects were to have a significant effect on the development of society in the future.

The new Methodism which quickly attracted large membership, especially in rural areas, offered the leaders enhanced ministerial status and greater freedom of action, and its members (a high proportion of the poor, initially) opportunities for social mobility through following religious precepts. By 1800 'there was a sudden acceleration, a broadening of a sectarian cult into something like a national faith' (Kiernan, quoted in Hill). Methodism had wide appeal because it was separate from the established Church of England, which was regarded by many as apathetic, lacking dynamism and relevance; it was also seen to embody a new progressive, evangelising radical spirit. It attracted membership through the powers of its charismatic preachers, who advocated egalitarian and ecumenical values. Its organising body is known as Conference.

POINTS OF EVALUATION

1 Critics of the concept of a typology (especially Stark and Bainbridge) claim that it is hard to make really clear distinctions and that to try to do so merely adds to confusion. For example, it is difficult to see at what exact point Methodism became a Denomination and at what point it might become a Church or return to being a sect.
2 There remains a tendency for analysis to be undertaken in terms of Christian examples.

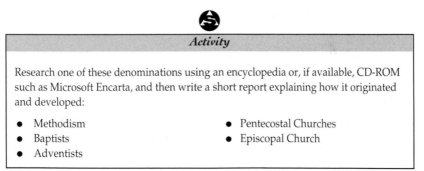

Activity

Research one of these denominations using an encyclopedia or, if available, CD-ROM such as Microsoft Encarta, and then write a short report explaining how it originated and developed:

- Methodism
- Baptists
- Adventists
- Pentecostal Churches
- Episcopal Church

SECTS AND CULTS

THE ORIGIN OF SECTS AND CULTS

The western world was dominated by the Catholic Church until the Reformation, when Protestantism and other new **sects** began to emerge. Some grew rapidly attracting many dissenters, people discontented with the Churches. Religious persecutions followed, until greater tolerance of the plurality of religious organisations was gained, although the Church of England was the established, State religion. Sociologists have subsequently undertaken ways of analysing the reasons for the changes and the differences between types.

- **Troeltch** contrasted the concept of a sect with that of a church. He developed a continuum between the conservative church and the perfectionist sect.
- **Neibuhr** argued that sects gradually evolve into denominations over time if they do not collapse through lack of support.
- **Yinger** included in his typology a category defined as 'established sects', those which survive by establishing clear distinctions between themselves and the rest of society. For example, the Plymouth Brethren; the Amish and the Mennonites (but see p 93).
- **Stark and Bainbridge** use the concept of relative deprivation in their analysis of the origin of sects. They argue that people who feel relatively deprived (lacking the material goods and social status of others with whom they compare themselves), or because of inferior status, alienated from established religion tend to be attracted to sects. Sect membership may provide them with greater equality and democratic opportunities.
- **Wilson** argues that sects are most likely to originate in periods of sudden or rapid social change. The universe of meaning and the plausibility structures which people have established become undermined. Social disruption calls for new methods of coping; sects answer such needs. He defines sects as 'ideological movements having as their explicit and declared aim the maintenance, and perhaps even the propagation of certain ideological positions'.

For example:

1 Pentecostalist sects have been especially popular among West Indian immigrants in Britain (see also p 115).
2 Black Muslims in the USA were attracted to a sect which offered salvation from white oppression and became a major political motivating force in the 1960s and 70s.

- **Bruce** argues that sects are significant because they are 'the greenhouse of faith; some members are retained, some are lost to denominations and some to the secular world'.

Whereas sociologists have developed a typology of church, sect and denomination, the concept of the **cult** is an additional form that requires analysis. They have been examined in terms of the emergence of New Religious Movements. All major religions began as **cults**, including Buddhism, Islam and Christianity. They are movements having no connections with existing religions within the society, although they may relate to those of other societies. Sects, on the other hand, are organisations which have broken away from an existing religion within the society. Their characteristics can be compared and contrasted.

Table 9: *Comparing sects and cults*		
	SECTS	CULTS
Structure and leadership	Lack bureaucratic structure; no hierarchy of power and few paid officials. Normally led by a charismatic leader who claims to be divinely informed. Critical of established religion; aim to re-establish fundamental truths. Neibuhr said they are short-lived and face survival problems. Success depends on recruiting more devoted members. If they grow very large they change into denominations (as Methodists and Baptists did). Wilson says survival depends on beliefs. Adventist sects (predicting the end of the world) have survived a long time by remaining highly exclusive.	Lack bureaucratic structure, are typically short-lived. If they survive and grow, they become sects. Normally have charismatic leaders, claiming special knowledge. Seldom any paid officials or hierarchical structure. Stark and Bainbridge describe three types of cult: 1 Cult movements: well organised; provide literature, meetings and guidance; eg Scientology. 2 Audience cults: lack structure. Members share a general interest; eg yoga; astrology; meditation. 3 Client cults: offer a service or therapy to members for a fee; eg EST.
Relations with wider society	Endeavour to protect members from influences of the secular world; make use of special books, films and music. Some become well accepted by wider society; eg **Mormons** (founded 1847, British membership 17,000. First Temple 1950, now 40 others in the world); **Jehovah's Witnesses** (founded 1872, increasing membership. Occasional conflict with the State over refusal to do military service or allow blood transfusions).	Frequently in conflict with wider society. Often advocate behaviour seen as 'deviant' or 'bizarre'. This can result in a moral panic (brainwashing members); eg, in 1981 **Bhagwan Shree Rajneesh** spent $6 million in building a spiritual community for 'an experiment in spiritual communism'; in 1981, Moonies lost a libel case in UK – described as 'a sinister, immensely wealthy, multi-national organisation, which brainwashed youngsters, broke up families and left parents in despair'.
Beliefs and services	See themselves as an elect or elite and believe they hold a monopoly of religious truths. Insist on strict loyalty of members; have powers of expulsion. Services vary from highly meditative (**Quakers**), to long and unstructured (**Snake Sects** of USA; members bring poisonous snakes and handle them as evidence that the truly faithful will not be	Tend not to have acts of public worship, and have few collective rituals. No clearly defined theology; usually a diffusion (syncretism) of religious ideas. **Transcendental Meditation** (TM) embodies Hindu ideas; **Cargo Cults** (see p 13) embody Christian beliefs; many cults offer unusual beliefs based on the ideas of the charismatic leader

	harmed). Services last many hours, during which people may speak in tongues. Sect meetings may often be highly emotional with much singing and dancing in which some enter hypnotic trances.	(L. Ron Hubbard, Founder of Scientology, wrote science fiction books). 1979: 900 members of **The People's Temple** committed suicide on the instructions of its leader. 1997: 30 members of **Heavens Gate** committed suicide to allow their souls to be carried away by a passing comet.
Membership	Exclusive: people request membership. They accept the strong barriers that exist between sect and wider society. There are distinctions between members and non-members. Membership in UK of all sects is about 5% of the adult population. They are required to adhere strictly to the doctrines. Membership can be gained by conversion experience. Weber said that sect membership was strongest among the materially deprived or those facing discrimination. Distinctiveness is sometimes achieved through special dress or appearance.	Voluntary; the most loosely-knit of all religious organisations. Membership numbers are impossible to calculate because no regular attendance is required; people move in and out of them. Normally oppose values of wider society (which is their attraction). Concerned with an experience of an emotional, mystical or therapeutic kind. New cults often appear in places where there has been social upheaval, rapid social change or great social fluidity. Members are attracted by the explanations they offer (see p 81).
Values	Tend to be radical; do not support the status quo; may represent non-conformist thinking, and often emerge from a schism within larger organisations which have abandoned traditional beliefs. This can lead to attacks on secular culture (TV, films, books). May also be in conflict with the State where there is a conflict of values. Aspire to inward perfection.	Tend to be in greater conflict with mainstream society than sects. Their members often adopt new lifestyles, resulting in a change in identity. They are often accused of subjecting members to psychological (sometimes physical) abuse and are then 'adopted' by their cult 'family'. This can be seen as a total institution where it provides for every need. They often aspire to a hostile orientation to other institutions.
Power	Hold strong power over members because they are subject to test of merit. Expulsion can follow. Some engage in psychological controls through encounter groups, which criticise and rebuild personalities. Have little or no interest in wider political power; members see their	Cult movements have greater power over followers than audience or client cults, and are sometimes subject to legal battles to retrieve family members. Some cult movements (especially those associated with New Age or New Social Movements) may have political influence. Those

	ultimate fate in the hands of God, not politicians.	associated with special issues, such as gay rights, animal rights and environmental issues may influence government policy.
Attractions	Often appeal to young people who feel anomic, vulnerable and uncertain. They are offered a father figure (leader), supportive friends (a family), economic support, clear moral guidelines and a set of clear answers about the future. They also have a theology which defines underprivilege as a sign of worth. People obtain a new dignity often denied them in wider society	The new and strange ideas can be attractive. Henslin said 'a cult is a new or different religion, whose teachings and practices put it at odds with the dominant culture and religion'. For the dispossessed, the cult may offer the knowledge that their status and lifestyle will change rapidly when the prophecies are fulfiled. People may turn to the charismatic leader for special insights. The **Moonies** (Unification Church) recruits through 'love bombing', to give a feeling of community.

Study point

Weber said that sects appeal to people from the marginal, lower classes. Do you think is the case?

TYPES OF SECT

Wilson argued that sects develop and change; they are not static entities, but are diverse and complex. They are attempts by people to construct their own societies, forging new normative patterns to fit with their ideologies, which are usually in opposition to those of wider, secular society. He emphasises eight special qualities which relate to a sect membership:

1 voluntary
2 exclusive
3 based on merit
4 a source of identity

5 elite identity
6 expulsion is possible
7 individual conscience is vital
8 members must accept the sect as legitimate

He classified sects according to their response to the world. The principal criterion is their response to the question 'what shall we do to be saved'? He noted that different types of sect made different types of appeal, and said the categories must not be from the Christian tradition alone nor from only a particular period in history. On this basis he identified seven types and the fundamental message they offered.

1 **Revolutionist:** 'God will overturn the world'; the present order will disappear and the chosen people will become powerful. They are most common in developing societies. Example: Rastafarians.
2 **Introvertionist:** 'God calls us to abandon the world'. The chosen people must cut themselves off from the secular world and follow a spiritual way of life. Examples: Plymouth Brethren; Mennonites; Amish.
3 **Reformist:** 'God calls us to amend the world'; the alterations are revealed to those open to supernatural influence. Example: Quakers.

THE QUAKERS WERE ESTABLISHED IN 1652 IN THE UK, AND HAVE ABOUT 18,000 MEMBERS. WHY HAS THIS RELIGION SURVIVED FOR SO LONG WITHOUT BECOMING A DENOMINATION?

4 **Utopian:** 'God calls us to reconstruct the world'. They withdraw from the secular world and build their own spiritual communitarian society. Example: The People's Temple.
5 **Convertionist:** 'God will change us'. These are evangelical sects whose members crusade to save souls who are in danger of eternal damnation. They hold meetings, and constantly seek new supporters. For Wilson, this is the type, like the early Methodists, which is most likely to turn into a denomination. Examples: Pentacostalists; Jehovah's Witnesses.

6 **Manipulationist:** 'God calls us to change our perceptions'. They see the need to be active in the world in which spiritual communal values have been weakened. They emphasise the need for bodily health, to abstain from harmful substances. They are not so concerned with salvation for a life after death, which is taken for granted. Example: Salvation Army.

7 **Thaumaturgical:** 'God will grant dispensations'. He will continue to express his presence through miracles, spiritual messages and healing. Examples: Spiritualists; Christian Science.

Points of evaluation

- Wilson is aware that the categories he suggests (like any others devised) can never describe every sect with precision in the terms of the category into which it is placed.
- The aim is to make a model, not to describe reality. This should help researchers when they look at new sects to see how it approximates to others in terms of beliefs, values, structure and so on.
- It is also important to remember that sects undergo changes, and therefore the categorisation of them must be flexible to allow for this.

Activity
Ernst Troeltsch developed Max Weber's ideas and made a distinction between church and sect. Tabulate six key differences between a church and a sect (see p 65).

NEW RELIGIOUS MOVEMENTS

Throughout history there have been examples of groups which place emphasis on mystical or other beliefs which are not easily susceptible to scientific testing. Many such groups (not always Christian in basis) have become more prominent in recent times, since they have attracted many eminent people as supporters or advocates. These have become known as **New Religious Movements** (NRMs). Closely associated with them are New Age Movements and New Social Movements. Most have the form of cults; those that survive may become sects.

Roy Wallis analysed the NRMs which emerged in the 1960s and 70s. Some were transient and others (with a stronger religious base often imported from Eastern religions) tended to attract young people. They involved new attitudes to morality, dress, and lifestyle, and were frequently supported by new music, eminent pop stars and others who could act as role models. They included:

- **ISKON** (International Society for Krishna Consciousness)
- **The Jesus People** and **The Children of God:** making use of some Christian doctrines

- **The Divine Light Mission; Transcendental Meditation**: both based on Indian mysticism
- **The Moonies**: based mainly on a mix of Eastern religions, and politically rightwing; led by a Korean business man, Sun Myung Moon, who was credited with being the Messiah. Eileen Barker analysed this organisation, and concluded that most members are not coerced; they come from middle class homes and seek a strong sense of security in their lives. They believe they can serve the Moonie community as effectively as their parents in their society.
- **Scientology:** based on psychological self-help therapeutic philosophies, with a mystical dimension. Its claim was to eliminate psychological illness, increase IQ, improve career opportunities and allow the individual to recover lost spiritual powers. The charges for such insights are very high. In 1997 German courts ruled that it should be excluded from Germany; it is not recognised as a religion.
- **EST** (Erhard Seminars Training): offered a shorter period of training, at the end of which, lives would be transformed. Such movements make use of current aspects of psychology and related disciplines, and claim that the insights can be used to enable people to achieve perfection and achieve an inner divine nature.

Many of these groups act more like businesses than religious organisations, employing the techniques of modern marketing and advertising to attract members. Wallis argues that it is helpful to develop a typology so that different types of NRN can be categorised according to their characteristics.

World-affirming religions
Examples: Transcendental Meditation, Scientology, EST.

They have more in common with cults, since they have little direct basis in any major religion. They provide insights which relate more to psychology and psychotherapy. They generally require no special place of worship, and offer training at a high cost.

World-accommodating new religious movements
Examples: Neo-Pentacostalism and the Charismatic groups found among the denominations.

These offer some stronger direct experience of God, including a belief that the Holy Spirit can touch congregations, enable members to speak in tongues (thought to be angelic language) and experience ecstatic revelations.

World-rejecting new religious movements
Examples: ISKON and The Children of God, The People's Temple; The Moonies, which profoundly reject the secular world.

They respond more like traditional introvertionist sects. The outside world is seen as corrupt and beyond redemption. Such groups teach that there is to be a spiritual revolution and members will be the saved. Commitment is usually total.

The origins of the NRMs

Wallis argues that the increasing process of scientific rationalisation in daily and social life during the 1960s and 70s provides the backdrop to the emergence of the NRMs. Young people in particular often reacted to alienating and dehumanising experiences of work, breakdown in family life and limited economic opportunities, by turning to one of the NRMs.

- The world-affirming religions offered ways of coping with the aspirations for status, power and personal attractiveness. They provided advice on how to cope with the ideals. Others gave advice on how to remain in the everyday world and still attain insights about the inner self. These attracted the more middle class membership.

- World-rejecting sects tended to attract those for whom the counter culture of the 1960s had failed, and frequently their message was to reject the materialist world in favour of the spiritual life.

- World-accommodating sects developed because the members were disillusioned with the established Churches, and they wished to get back to central doctrines of purity.

Many of the NRMs underwent major change (especially the world-rejecting sects) as members drifted away. Some adopted more conventional approaches to the world or found the basis for support elsewhere. Some have been subject to strong media attack (such as Scientology) and been unable to develop. Others accommodated to the world to such an extent that they have disappeared.

Wallis sees the significance of these NRMs in terms of the preoccupation.

'with searching for a remedy to cope with the world as it is or for a transformation of it into a utopia. Such movements take new forms in each new historical and cultural location, appealing to different social groups and initiated by different social circumstances'.

The Sociology of New Religions, 1985

Points of evaluation

It is always difficult to establish categories for analysis. Sects and cults often show high levels of complexity in beliefs and behaviour. For example, it is difficult to identify the Mormon type. The Mormons may appear to be world-affirming, providing followers with positive ways of coping with the world, but world-rejecting insofar as they form a select community in Utah, make use of their own holy book (The Book of Mormon), have advocated polygamy and believe in baptism by proxy. They have elements of being world-accommodating in that they wish to regain a lost spirituality for members (including the dead). On the other hand, Wallis's ideas add more insights and offer refinements to previous approaches.

NEW AGE MOVEMENTS

Grace Davie suggests that the **New Age Movement** 'is a phenomenon that affirms the continuing significance of the sacred in contemporary society but in far from conventional forms'. She explains that the term includes a wide range of issues that involve advocates of alternative medicine, environmental movements, ways of stimulating business managers into better practice and philosophies about new therapies: 'It is a rich amalgam of philosophies and practices (from both eastern and Western traditions), involving contrasting groups of people in a wide variety of places'. Their emergence raises questions for Christianity, and there are unusual ways suggested for achieving 'the wholeness of the individual'.

She concludes that generally, they are alternatives to and rivals of conventional religiosity. They do not share a common core of belief and practice with mainstream Churches; 'Like the customer of a self service cafeteria, the seeker puts together a package of supernatural beliefs and practices.' These may constantly change as new ideas enter their horizon of experimentation; 'To get the new age in perspective one must appreciate the transient and selective nature of much involvement in it.' Davie notes that British society is changing in its structure and organisation; consumption is becoming the dominant mode of economic organisation as we enter a period of postmodernity. There are changes in patterns of employment, in housing, and in the choices which people have about how to conduct their lives. These affect their opportunities for partners, leisure pursuits, education and establishing a lifestyle from all the options.

All religions are faced with questions about how best to promote their aspirations for influence in the lives of people and how to combat the forces which undermine such aims. Social groups which could be targeted include elderly people (Britain has an ageing population). There is a new plurality of ethnic groups, each with their own needs and expectations, most of which serve to promote a growth in religious activity.

Davie suggests that it is important to analyse New Age Movements: 'They can provide us with a powerful lens through which to view the wider society...' She implies that their presence enable researchers to understand more about changing values and aspirations, and the ways people search for meanings.

Beckford agrees that the controversies generated by New Age and New Religious Movements become 'the barometers of changes taking place in a number of different societies'.

Points of evaluation

1 Critics see New Age Movements in negative ways, promoting weird cults which offer irrational belief systems, having no supporting body of theological knowledge, or having a basis in unconventional psychology.
2 Proponents such as Beckford argue that the emerging movements reveal that the British are not altogether unfriendly towards religious diversity, although some organisations are better tolerated than others. He suggests that the problem that religion has in attracting membership is not unique; most voluntary groups have similar difficulties: 'The split between believing and belonging is therefore part of a broader pattern of change which happens to affect religious organisations amongst others.' In fact, the New Age Movements may be fertile ways of attracting more people to an interest in religious matters, and enable people to identity with the sacred.
3 Davie has said 'Industrialisation made the "church" impossible.' She suggests that the denomination is also in decline and the essence of true religious belief is increasingly to be found in sects and cults. It is here, she says that we can see 'the true believers inside their carefully constructed stockade and the cultic consumers constructing their individual lifestyles and options.'

THE ATTRACTION OF CULTS

Campbell (1972) suggests that all the new cult movements are part of a counter culture to which people turn who are opposed to mainstream orthodoxies. Beckford suggests that changes in religious practice and belief (as manifested in New Age Movements) must be looked at in relation to the changes going on in wider society. There is greater emphasis on leisure pursuits as technological changes affect working hours and incomes. Young people in particular search for new ways of expressing their ideals and their needs.

Some commentators suggest that:

- The occasion of the year 2000 will encourage more bizarre groups to emerge to offer a new spiritual enlightenment and predictions about the end of the world.
- The end of the communist empire in 1989 disillusioned many people about the possibility of a socialist utopia, and caused some to turn to religious forms of community. There are reports of new millennial cults in parts of Russia, which are attracting large numbers of followers.

- The internet has also opened up the possibilities of an expansion of cult groups, ideal for the quick recruitment of new congregations.
- Evangelical television programmes have strong support, as well as programmes about the supernatural.
- There are growing numbers of therapy cults advocating unusual psychological ways of coping with the stress of life.

POSSIBLE DANGERS OF CULT MOVEMENTS

1 Such movements are often criticised for the methods by which they obtain and hold members.
2 They are often led by charismatic leaders who can induce dangerous behaviour in followers.
   a In 1978, more than 900 members of a cult, The People's Temple, committed suicide under the instructions of the leader Jim Jones. They were mainly comparatively poor people.
   b In 1993, 80 people died in a gun battle with police at Waco in Texas. They were members of the Branch Davidians, and many members were wealthy and educated.
   c Since 1994, 74 members of The Order of the Solar Temple have been involved in violent deaths in Canada, Switzerland and France. They believe that they will reign in a serene state forever on the star Sirius.
   d In 1997, 39 members of the cult, Heaven's Gate, committed suicide in Santa Fe. They claimed that they would be reincarnated on the Comet Hale-Bopp which was passing at its closest point to the earth at that time (similar cults emerged in 1911 when Halley's comet passed the earth.) This cult has characteristics of a Millenarian Movement. Members predicted the end of the world on their website. Many of its small membership were well educated and well off.

Activity

Read the details relating to the cult known as Aum Shinrikyo and suggest reasons why it might attract a following in Russia; why it might be a short-lived cult and under what circumstances it could develop into a sect.

Shoko Asahara, whose cult has an office in Moscow, claims to have reigned during past lives as king of heaven, where unidentified flying objects come from. He has announced plans to establish an astral hospital using astral medicine from the astral world. He has established a large following for his cult, Aum Shinrikyo, and has warned them that the apocalypse is due to occur soon, when the world will be destroyed. He has told them that he will act as their defence lawyers on Judgement day. Only if they redouble their devotion to his teaching can he hope to save them. Millennial cults are prone to violence because of their belief that a catastrophic war or huge disaster will cause them to enter paradise. The more extreme millennialists isolate disciples and subject them to ever greater tests of devotion and endurance.

Adapted from Newsweek report April 13th 1995

Study point

Do you think that all cults are necessarily deviant organisations? Give examples for and against. Under what conditions might a cult become labelled as deviant?

MEDIA COVERAGE OF RELIGION

MORAL PANICS

Information about NRMs frequently appears in the media, because the stories often involve bizarre events. The outcome is that the public develops a great concern about the behaviour which is thought to be dangerous or deviant, and often involves young people. The stories serve to sensitise the public and develop their expectations; they warn them to expect that other similar behaviour will follow in the near future. The ending of the old millennium and the onset of the new is especially potent. Images and stereotypes of the participants emerge. These fit into the news values of the popular press, which invariably cover stories which meet their specialist formula of sex, shock and sensation.

EVANGELICAL TELEVISION

Steve Bruce examines the ways that religion is dealt with in the media (especially television) and considers the ways that evangelists have made use of television to propagate their ideas.

- The media show more interest in the exotic religious world than their membership figures would seem to deserve.
- The high profile of a number of television evangelists during the Reagan

presidency (1980–88) attracted the attention of social scientists who supposed the New Christian Right to be a powerful political force.
- Recent changes in British broadcasting legislation has made it possible for new evangelising television programmes in Britain. They will set out to recruit support for a particular religious group or ideology. This worries mainstream British religious groups who hold a wider ecumenical view and oppose fundamentalism.

There are many problems in examining the effects of television (whether on violence, sexual attitudes or religious beliefs). Researchers have not finally established whether watching television produces a major change it intends, a change not intended, reinforces what already exists or prevents some change that would otherwise have occurred. There is evidence that television does not have a strong independent effect; it is too easily ignored, talked over or switched off, and people perceive selectively. The main effect is therefore confirmation that Television messages influence only the sympathetic.

EVALUATION

1 Television evangelism is perceived as a threat by some critics, who argue that sophisticated programme-makers can appear to establish a personal bond with the audience, who may be particularly susceptible to their messages. But this may be unfounded. In Britain less than 5 per cent of people are evangelical, compared with 25 per cent in USA.
2 Some people argue that such programmes are more likely to be preaching to the converted, and are merely reinforcing existing views.
3 There is also the entertainment value they offer which may provide some element of spiritual values, but is unlikely to be very influential.

Activity
Monitor local and national newspapers for a week to examine the ways in which stories relating to religion are discussed. Enter details under the following headings:

NEWSPAPER	HEADLINE	PAGE	DATE	NEWS VALUES REVEALED (does the story cover sex; sensation; bizarre?)	BRIEF DETAILS

MILLENARIAN MOVEMENTS

The term 'millenarian' has been taken from the prophesy in the Bible describing the thousand year reign of Christ, the millennium. Wilson notes that in the Christian tradition millenarians are groups which emphasise the second advent of Christ: 'They believe that the occasion will be associated with the divine intervention in the affairs of man by the overthrowing of social and physical order.' They feature frequently in the history of Christian churches, where leaders have emerged attracting followings of poor or oppressed people based on their prophecies of the end of the world or the imminent collapse of society and its transformation.

Such movements share the view of revolutionary sects that the world will be reborn through supernatural means in the foreseeable future; the world of the gods and of man will merge and a new social system will appear; believers will be saved and transformed so that they will no longer suffer pain or deprivation. For Jehovah's Witnesses, there are just 144,000 of the elect to be saved.

In less developed societies, such movements are related to colonial intervention in social life, especially where there has been a Judeo-Christian-Muslim input into the culture. In these cases, Wilson explains, millennialism is often associated with the restoration of the physical, social and cultural conditions of the past. In this respect it differs from the millennialism of Christian sects which describe a new heaven on earth or an assumption of believers into heaven. Such movements in pre-industrial societies are associated with means of restoring the past, warfare, rebellion, independence movements and also with more basic economic issues. These include how to obtain scarce resources which the western world seem to have in abundance but which are of limited availability in their own society. The demand of millenarianism is the transformation of the social situation in which people find themselves; they want new economic and status opportunities.

EXAMPLE OF A MILLENARIAN MOVEMENT: THE VAILALA CULT

Worsely describes the outbreak of Vailala Madness, which broke out in 1919 in Papua New Guinea. The cult had developed following the work of missionaries, who brought elements of their western culture, including the artifacts for building and mechanical devices for constructing boats, unknown in those areas. The madness started when a native went into a trance, had visions of deceased kinsmen and ancestors, and gave prophecies of the coming of a steamer with a cargo for the natives.

This gave rise to a cult based on the idea that the native people would inherit valuable resources from the ancestors, based on European culture. Their idea of heaven included the fact that they would wear long colourful robes of the catholic missionaries. Elements of Christian ethics were built into their beliefs. Painted flagpoles became the features of the cult in villages, which it was later suggested were imitations of the Persian Oil Company's wireless aerials. In each village where the cult operated, a temple was established called a hot house, associated with the power of men from the past. A long pole was kept in each temple and from it messages were said to be received from ancestors. The pole was also accredited with special healing powers. The cult was marked by mass giddiness, when individuals would sway and utter gibberish. This was associated with visions of the ancestors, who promised the return of valuable cargoes containing tobacco, calico, knives, axes and foodstuffs.

The cult was seen as a powerful expression of the expectations and demand for the transformation of native life. Calling on the ancestors was an attempt to destroy the traditional ways and establish new rituals of greater power, which would facilitate the arrival of the valued cargoes that only the Europeans seemed to obtain and enjoy. Worsley sees such cargo cults as a spontaneous outburst of feelings against oppression being organised within a 'rational' ideology. The Vailala Madness was an attempt to absorb new information about western technology, to wish into being a new order of affluence and new opportunities for status, based on the powers of ancestors, who were the protectors of the community in the past. This, like other cults, disappeared when major events passed and the prophecies of the leaders failed.

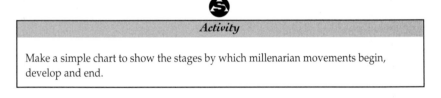

Activity

Make a simple chart to show the stages by which millenarian movements begin, develop and end.

Points of evaluation

1 Worsley sees some evidence for the Marxist view of religion in the ways in which millennarian movements develop as responses to exploitation by powerful groups. He says 'the class struggle is exported to the colonies and race differences become surrogates of relationships between the classes.'

2 The concept of relative deprivation is a useful one in the analysis of such movements. The people displayed feelings of deprivation when confronted with a more affluent lifestyle.

3 Millenarian movements may also emerge for other reasons, including the imposition of new technologies and economic methods of production, and the introduction of new political structures.

Copy table 10 onto an A3 size sheet of paper. Complete the details required in each box. Keep a copy of the completed table in your file for future reference and revision.

Table 10: *Religious organisations*				
FEATURE	CHURCH	DENOMINATION	SECT	CULT
Scope	National (or international); Very large membership inclusive	National (or international); large membership	Local (or national) Exclusive	Local; exclusive; small membership
Internal organisation				
Life span				
Attitude to wider society				
Attitude to other religious groups				
Attitude to members				
Type of membership				
Social background of members				
Examples (4 for each type)				

$$STUDY \quad \triangle \quad GUIDES$$

Group activities

Undertake a short joint project. Group members to establish:

- The number of different churches, denominations, sects, cults, NRMs or New Social Movements which operate within a 20 mile radius, and how long they have been in existence.
- Their membership structure; average attendance and type of leadership (priest, vicar, pastor).
- The views of a sample of the public regarding these organisations.

Key Concepts Activity

Each group to define and discuss the terms listed on p 63, with examples from their own experience. Write the definition on a Key Concept Card for revision purposes (see p 3).

Practice questions

1 'The Church's beliefs and values tend to be conservative and support the established social, political and economic order in the society of which it is part'. Discuss.
2 Examine some of the explanations that sociologists have put forward for the emergence of new religious movements in recent years. What attempts have been made to understand their structure and significance?
   a   Briefly outline what sociologists mean by the term 'Church'.
   b   Identify and describe what sociologists have seen as the key features of religious denominations.
   c   Discuss the major similarities and differences between the sects and cults.

Coursework suggestions

1 Research one new religious movement. Describe its central beliefs. Using the list of characteristic headings for churches, sects, denominations and cults (pp 65–70), complete similar details for your chosen movement.
2 There has been a developing interest in recent years in alien life, reflected in television programmes and films such as *Independence Day*, *Men in Black*, *The X-Files*. Undertake a study to see how viewers assess them as explanations for the mysterious.
3 Sample a population of young people (15–25 years old) and establish their attitudes towards mainstream religious organisations, sects and cults. Are there differences by class, gender or ethnicity?

6

SECULARISATION

Introduction

THIS CHAPTER LOOKS at the various definitions of secularisation and outlines the arguments for and against the view that religion is in decline.

Table 11: *Theorists, concepts and issues in this chapter*		
KEY THEORIST	KEY CONCEPTS	KEY ISSUES
Bryan Wilson	Secularisation	• The origins of secularisation
Larry Shiner	Desacrilisation Disengagement	• The meaning of secularisation
David Martin	Subterranean theologies	
Will Herberg	Civic religion	• The arguments for and against secularisation
Rodney Stark	Cultural defence	• Explanation for secularisation in Britain
William Bainbridge	Cultural transition	
Robert Bellah	Individuation	
Thomas Luckmann	Privatisation of religion Invisible religion	
Talcott Parsons	Structural differentiation	
Max Weber	Disenchantment Demystification	

One of the issues which interests sociologists is the apparent persistence of religion over long periods of time in all societies. Religion seems to survive various environments, including extreme persecution, and societies in which there is high level of scientific understanding of the world. It may seem paradoxical that in such societies there have also developed many *new* religious movements which challenge the existing churches for membership. This has led sociologists to find ways of assessing the strength of the religious belief and behaviour, and to see if there is a strengthening process of **secularisation**.

THE ORIGINS OF SECULARISATION

The growth of secularism from the nineteenth century was influenced by eminent thinkers in the fields of natural and social science such as Comte, Darwin, Marx and Freud. They had a great impact on the way in which people thought about the origin of the species, and the place of religion in their lives. At a time of rapid development of science and the growth of empiricism, religious explanations were no longer taken for granted; the process of enlightenment and modernity encouraged people to question religious doctrines.

Weber and Durkheim believed that religion would be undermined (though not necessarily eradicated) in a new rational society. Other institutions would provide the sources of solidarity and the means of achieving valued goals. The social historian Toynbee stated that in the early part of the twentieth century, the great world religions had been replaced by three post-Christian ideologists: communism, nationalism and individualism. He was describing the growth of a secular world.

In every society the extent of secularisation exists along a continuum, from very weak to very strong. However, it has become a widely held view that western societies in particular have undergone very powerful processes of secularisation in recent times, as a result of modernisation.

THE MEANING OF SECULARISATION

Bryan Wilson defines secularisation as 'the process whereby religious thinking, practices and institutions lose social significance'. This involves the following features:

- The transference of religious powers and property to State control.
- The shift from religious to secular control of traditional activities and functions of religion.

- The decline in the proportion of time and resources which people devote to mystical concerns.
- The decay of religious institutions and religious consciousness.

Study point

Suggest ways in which you could research some of these features of secularisation.

Peter Berger defines secularisation as 'the process by which sectors of society and culture are removed from the domination of religious institutions and symbols'. He adds that apart from the secularisation of society and culture, there is also the 'secularisation of consciousness'. By this he means that in western societies 'there are an increasing number of people who look upon their own lives without the benefit of religious interpretation'.

Larry Shiner suggests that sociologists should be very careful about using the term secularisation because it lacks precision. Indeed, he asks 'what exactly is the index of secularisation? Is it church attendance? Belief in immortality? The amount of private prayer? The number of scientists who believe in God? Or is it some other form of religiosity?' He reviewed the uses of the term in research and found six different meanings to show how confused its users are:

1 The decline of religion
2 Conformity with this world
3 Disengagement
4 Transposition of religious beliefs and institutions
5 Desacrilisation
6 The movement from a sacred to a secular society.

THE DECLINE OF RELIGION

Argument: Previously accepted religious symbols, doctrines and institutions lose their prestige and influence, culminating in a society without religion. Attendances decline and beliefs become more liberal.

Evaluation

- It is difficult to establish the point in history when and where the decline started. Was there ever a 'golden age of religion' when the whole of Britain was truly Christian?
- The extent of clerical prestige, church attendance, use of prayer and so on depend on the use of valid questionnaires and other documentary evidence. Statistical data is always open to question. Who collected it, for what purpose and by what means?

THE CONFORMITY WITH THIS WORLD

Argument: Society turns its attention away from the supernatural and becomes more interested in 'this world'. Conventional religions are no longer the sources of ultimate meanings and values for the majority. There are other more important sources of belief systems (eg, political and secular ideologies).

Evaluation

The implication is that where this occurs, conventional religion is gradually lost because people no longer reflect its values in their daily lives. In fact, people may just have shifted the emphasis of their beliefs from the orthodox to the less orthodox.

DISENGAGEMENT

Argument: Religion loses most of its traditional functions. In the Middle Ages, the Church in union with the State had great wealth, powers of patronage and was a source of daily influence. In the twentieth century, it has lost many of its functions to specialised institutions such as schools, social services and the mass media. It becomes less influential in moral terms. Religion is relegated to the realm of the private.

Evaluation

Many major religions have survived persecution by religious groups maintaining the faith in secret. The religion then re-blossoms once the threat has retreated. It could do so in the West again. Parsons argues that the withdrawal of churches from non-religious functions is evidence of **structural differentiation** which does not equal secularisation; instead, they become more effective because they are purer, and can concentrate on spiritual activities.

THE TRANSPOSITION OF RELIGIOUS BELIEFS AND INSTITUTIONS

Argument: There is a transformation of religious knowledge, beliefs and institutions into non-religious forms. Ideas of progress, equality and individual responsibility which were once seen in religious terms, become accepted as secular ideologies. A political ideology may replace Christianity.

Evaluation

It is difficult to prove that secular ideologies necessarily developed from religious teaching.

DESACRILISATION

Argument: Traditional ways of thinking about the world which involved mystical, supernatural or religious explanations, are superseded by those based on scientific modes of thought. People become independent of religion in their daily lives, which they live by reason rather than by superstition and mystical explanations. Weber used the terms **disenchantment** and **demystification** to explain this process.

Evaluation

Even in a scientific society, a high proportion of the population continue to rely on mystical explanations, including luck, astrology, superstitions and other non-scientific methods of living out their daily lives (see table 2a, p 15).

THE MOVEMENT FROM A SACRED TO A SECULAR SOCIETY

Argument: There is a move from a simple society in which the sacred is central, to a complex, modern one in which religion plays an increasingly small part.

Evaluation

- Such usage is very generalised, implying an evolutionary change from traditional norms.
- There remains a problem of explaining the significance of **subterranean theologies** (beliefs in luck, charms, omens – see p 14) in modern societies which are not unlike those described in traditional ones.

CONCLUSION

Shiner concludes that even terms like religion could usefully be abandoned in favour of concepts like faith and tradition. As far as secularisation is concerned, the term has often served 'the partisans of controversy and has constantly taken on new meanings without completely losing the old ones'. As a result, 'the term is swollen with overtones and implications, especially those associated with indifference or hostility to whatever is considered religious'. If a more neutral term cannot be agreed, then he says everyone who uses it should state carefully their intended meaning, and stick to it.

Study points

To what extent do you agree that:

1 Religious symbols, doctrines and institutions have lost their prestige in contemporary society?
2 Contemporary society has turned its attention away from the supernatural and become more interested in 'this world'?
3 Religion has become mainly a matter of private reflection?

Activity
1   In small groups discuss Wilson's definition of secularisation (p 86). Present four arguments to oppose his views. 2   Briefly but clearly, define the following terms: **demystification, desacrilisation, disenchantment, disengagement**. 3   Write a dictionary entry for the term 'secularisation' (maximum 75 words).

ARGUMENTS FOR THE SECULARISATION THESIS

Bryan Wilson argues that religion has made way for scientific thought, reason and rational calculation.

His arguments, which illustrate and explain the loss in support for religion, are based on an analysis of church membership and attendance statistics, the decline in the institutional power of the church and the loss of influence of religious ideas and organisations. His understanding of what secularisation means can be seen in terms of Shiner's categories:

THE STATISTICS SHOWING 'DECLINE OF RELIGION'

All of the available statistics show a decline in membership and attendance in the 'traditional' churches. Table 12 shows that the high point for British church attendance and power was between about 1851–1951 when regular attendance among adult population was between 25–50 per cent (many people attended a service more than once on a Sunday). Such information comes from Church census data and by asking people about their religious behaviour in surveys. Both can be unreliable. In 1997, with attendance below 10 per cent, it was reported that the worldwide Anglican church was sending more missionaries to Britain than to any other member country, to find ways of rebuilding congregations.

Table 12: *Adult church attendance in England and Wales (1851-1989) (%)*										
	1851	1950	1955	1960	1965	1970	1975	1980	1985	1990
England/Wales	50	38	28	19	15	12	10	10	9	9
Scotland	60	50	40	25	22	20	18	15	12	

SOURCE: BRUCE, *RELIGION IN MODERN BRITAIN*

Table 13 shows that:

- attendance and membership of the two major churches has declined by more than 28 per cent between 1975–95.
- About 2.7 million people have stopped attending church in that time.
- Membership of other religious organisations (especially Methodist and Presbyterian denominations) has also fallen considerably.

Table 13: *Patterns of decline in attendance and membership (millions) 1975–95*		
ATTENDANCES/MEMBERSHIP	1975	1995
Church of England (electoral roll)	2.2	1.6
Roman Catholics (attendances)	2.4	1.7
Methodists (membership)	0.52	0.366
Presbyterian (membership)	1.4	0.99
No of adults regularly attending all churches	10.9	8.2

SOURCE: *UK CHRISTIAN HANDBOOK* 1997

Church attendance in general is predicted to fall to about 5 per cent unless there is a change in patterns of religious behaviour. There have been further declines in the use of Church marriages, baptisms, christenings, funerals and Sunday Schools (in 1902, 65 per cent of live births were baptised in the Church of England, but by 1993, this had fallen to 27 per cent). These figures support those who argue that the secularisation process is gathering pace; they argue that many religious organisations with the weakest support will disappear in the course of the twenty-first century.

Points of evaluation

Critics emphasise that while attendances figures show decline, other studies continue to show high levels of belief in the mystical, and at least nominal affiliation to mainstream churches. Also they note the exceptions to the pattern of secularisation, especially among:

- Baptists, whose numbers have much slower and more limited rates of decline.
- Pentacostal movements, the New Religious Organisations (charismatic house churches) and in Northern Ireland.
- different regional areas of England which show variations. The East Midlands, Humberside and Yorkshire show attendance at about 3 per cent, whereas parts of the West Country remain above 25 per cent.
- ethnic minority religions, most of which show increases in support.

RELIGIOUS DISENGAGEMENT

- The social and political power of the Church and clergy is in decline.
- The Churches have lost all moral control. They trim their values and beliefs to accommodate cultural and other social changes in attitude. They have made large concessions in terms of birth control, abortion, divorce and most other issues where once clear beliefs were held and enforced on members. Wilson argues that the 'content of the message that the churches seek to promote and the attitudes and values that it tries to encourage, no longer inform much of our national life'.
- The growth of mainly short-lived sects and cults is evidence of disengagement from traditional religious values.

CARDINAL HUME IS THE HEAD OF THE ROMAN CATHOLIC CHURCH IN UK. HOW HAS IT BEEN AFFECTED BY THE PROCESSES OF SECULARISATION?

PROCESS OF DESACRILISATION OF RELIGION

- Wilson suggests that for most people 'society appears to be dependent not on divine providence, but rather on social planning'.
- Many elements of modern society undermine traditional belief, especially mass media, new books (see p 97) and the growth of urban values.

INCREASING CONFORMITY WITH THIS WORLD

- Morality is seen as a relative matter.
- Secular values predominate; religious principles are largely irrelevant.

The analysis of the Amish sect, an agricultural community in Pennsylvania, supports the arguments relating to desacrilisation and increasing conformity, as an example of withdrawing from the secular world in order to retain traditional beliefs. However, recent analysis suggests that this, too, is failing. The Amish have separated themselves from modern society by refusing to allow members to have televisions, or any of the modern conveniences of life. They were founded by a Dutchman, Jakob Ammann, in the seventeenth century, who laid down strict rules about dress and behaviour; their first language is still Dutch, and they have, until recent times, managed to retain many traditional customs in the face of pressures which affected the majority of American citizens.

Allan Sim writes that in the context of the increasing secularisation of Western society, an image of the Amish persists as a group who are highly resistant to this change. In fact, he argues that the reality is somewhat different. While they are slow to change, they are not invulnerable to the secular forces which affect wider society. The Amish have divided into the Old Order (which seeks to maintain tradition) and the New Order, who are more open to accept change. However, many Amish who are now dealing in the tourist market are from both orders.

- They are unable to resist changes to their culture as a result of the commercial pressures inherent in modern society. Yet, they do not wish to convert others to their way of life since this might put them into close contact with outsiders.
- It is necessary for them to maintain the myth of separation for them to retain tourist interest.
- The secular world now threatens the Amish's traditional existence. Sim concludes with the question, 'if a culture as religiously centred as the Amish cannot resist the tide of secularisation, what chance does religion in our own culture stand?'

Points of evaluation

Wilson interprets every aspect of modern life as evidence of the power of secularisation.

- For him, a religious society has one church expressing one faith. New religious movements are described as 'no more than transient and volatile gestures of defiance'. As far as he is concerned, they are blind alleys in the search for community values.
- He sees the Churches as declining into sectarian status as the process of secularisation takes hold. People shop around for spiritual insights without having any serious long term interests in their philosophies, and take little notice of their doctrines.

Critics would argue that he is too dismissive of counter-evidence. For example, Berger agrees that secularisation is an undeniable process in modern society, but its consequences may not be as dire as those predicted by Wilson.

- Every society requires its plausibility structures (organised beliefs which help people make sense of their world, as a 'protective canopy' – see p 44). New sects may be evidence of secularisation, but, he argues, they are a protection for members from secularising influences. They provide new plausibility structures from which people can choose.

Will Herberg showed that in 1950s USA, religion lacked content, and had little to do with everyday life, other than to provide people with a sense of identity and drive. He examined the phenomenon of what appeared to be 'a notable turn to religion among the American people today'. He used statistics and reports to show the trend. One indicated that in the five years between 1949–53, the distribution of Scripture in USA increased 140 per cent; people were buying and distributing Bibles at an unprecedented rate. Over four-fifths of Americans said they believed the Bible 'to be the revealed word of God', rather than just 'a great piece of literature'. Yet more than 50 per cent of people sampled could not name any of the first four books of the New Testament. The picture he presented was of people lacking 'authentic religion' in their lives, even though they filled the churches.

It was his thesis that both the religiousness and the secularism of the American people derive from the same sources. He shows how it was necessary to belong to one of the three great faiths, Protestantism, Catholicism or Judaism, to be 'an American'. From the land of immigrants, he says, America became the 'triple melting pot', of the three great faiths. Religion became accepted as a normal part of The American Way of Life. Failure to identify with one of the three faiths implied being 'un-American' and disloyal. In 1955 President Eisenhower launched a 'back to God' campaign, saying 'without God there could be no American way of life'.

What Herberg describes in 1950s America, was the development of secularised religion.

- Americanism is the civic religion (the sanctification of society) of the American people.
- The unknown God of Americans seems to be faith itself; what Americans believe in when they say they are religious, is religion itself.
- He showed that there was an absence of God in the affairs of life, even though the churches were full.

Points of evaluation

1 Herberg's work was influential because it presented an understanding of how it is possible to be a regular churchgoer without necessarily being religious.

2 Bellah also later said that 'Faith in Americanism' provided the necessary loyalty to the nation.
3 Critics have suggested that Herberg's view is a dated one. In the intervening years, many new sects and cults have emerged and grown more rapidly than traditional churches and denominations. Melton has indicated that between 1960–1985, almost 500 new religious movements appeared in USA (of which about 60 became defunct). In the 1970s, the New Christian Right became a powerful force, making use of televangelism (see p 79) to attract support for traditional American values.
4 The question as to the nature of 'authentic religion' is open to debate. It is likely that it has always been the case that few regular churchgoers have a detailed knowledge of their faith.

Study point

Evaluate the strengths of these views:

1 Wilson: religion is in decline because people have lost their sense of what it means to be truly religious.
2 Herberg: it is functional for people to identify with a religious group even without real belief.

EXPLANATIONS FOR SECULARISATION IN BRITAIN

INDUSTRIALISATION

Industrialisation is seen as the dominant secularising process, which causes people to question traditional values. It epitomises the power of science to change the world; it is a source of increased affluence, making people's lives more secure; it allows people to have more free time, to read more widely, and question assumptions taken for granted by previous generations. It can lead to a crisis of credibility in religion.

SOCIAL CHANGES

1 Social and geographical mobility mean that whereas people used to live most of their lives in a local community in which the church played a leading role, populations have dispersed towards towns and cities, and church attendances have declined. Shared values have been lost.
2 As church attendance figures dropped, it became less the norm for children to be socialised into attending church and adopting religious family values.

3 Aldous Huxley, the eminent novelist and scientist, wrote in 1965,

> *'God isn't compatible with machinery and scientific medicine and universal happiness. You must make your choice. Our civilisation has chosen machinery, medicine and happiness'.*

This led to the increased fragmentation of society, differentiated with new classes and status groups. The dominant religions began to change with the advent of a socially mobile and more politically aware population. Protestantism divided into smaller factions; new denominations and sects emerged.

4 The emergence of new religions, and the competition of other groups for allegiance, meant that the chances of believing in any one of them became limited. Wilson said that 'once anonymity and impersonality became the dominant experience of man in western society, so Christianity, like any institutionalised religion, lost its grip on culture.'

RATIONALISATION

1 Modern societies emphasise the use of scientific logic and rationality rather than religion to address and solve social problems.

2 Whereas once it was the Church which controlled every rite of passage through life (supervising birth, baptism, marriage and death), other professions have taken over this function for the great majority of people. Turner argues that in everyday life, people turn to medical practitioners for advice about diet and other matters of bodily health, whereas these were once directed by religious principles; 'the doctor has replaced the priest.'

THE WELFARE STATE

The growth of the welfare state removed many of the tasks that used to be performed by religious institutions, especially health care, education, and social welfare. This helped to reduce the significance of religion on people's lives.

THE DEVELOPMENT OF THE MASS MEDIA

1 The expansion of the media, particularly television, has replaced the Church as the main source of authority and knowledge. Opinions are now more easily formed on the basis of media information than from a priest, although in some areas, such as Northern Ireland, such leaders may still be influential.

2 Wilson believes that the development of a powerful mass media has resulted in a diverse and relatively disordered knowledge. There has been a loss of absolutes in the lives of people, so that 'modern man lives in a random supermarket of knowledge that is in fact a maze'.

NEW PHILOSOPHIES

1 The increase in political and social philosophies which oppose (or provide alternatives to) the major Churches has had an undermining effect over time as the ideas have become part of wider social thought. As a result, there has been a growth in material values as opposed to spiritual ones.

2 There has been a collapse in the plausibility structures once imposed by religious institutions and their definitions of reality, as a result of new philosophies and new pressure on people in everyday life. In a modern pluralistic society, different religious, political and other groups committed to particular ideals are tolerated by the State and allowed to engage in free competition for membership. This means that people are confronted by a wide range of organisations, some religious, some secular (like trade unions and various clubs), all competing for their time and support. The pressure to attend a church is no longer likely to take precedence over the Sunday football or netball team.

Controversial books written by theologians

- **Dietrich Bonhoeffer** – *Letters and Papers from Prison* (1953)
  He was a German theologian who wrote of the need for a non-religious understanding of God. As people come of age, they can discard the idea of a father in heaven and accept that secularisation is part of God's plan to free men and women from a sense of subservience to Him. In fact, 'God is dead'.

- **Revd John Robinson** – *Honest To God* (1963)
  As Bishop of Woolwich, he wrote that in a modern secular age we need a less traditional religious approach; Christianity must divest itself of mysticism, abandon the idea of a 'God out there' and develop a new Christian ethic based on a social humanistic morality.

- **Revd Don Cupitt** – *The Time Being* (1995)
  He was Dean Emmanuel College Cambridge when he wrote that we need to have a reinvented religion, a 'kind of Green Christian humanism perhaps, or maybe the sort of mix of Buddhism, environmentalism and new therapies that is already familiar on the Alternative scene ... if religion is to have a future.'

- **Father Tissa Balasuriya** – *Mary and Human Liberation* (1997)
  He is a Catholic priest, declared by the Pope to be a threat to the church. He wrote that if it is to survive in Asia, Christianity must start a dialogue with other faiths and present its doctrines in more relevant ways. He questions the idea of original sin, and advocates greater social activism by the church, on behalf of the poor. This is important because the membership of the Catholic Church in the third world has overtaken the number in the west. He claims that Mary's support for her son Jesus makes her Catholicism's first priest.

Study point
Suggest why the books listed above might serve to undermine traditional religious beliefs.

GENERAL DISILLUSIONMENT

1 People feel disillusioned with mainstream churches, claiming they do not move with the times.
2 There are frequent scandals, crises and disputes which have torn churches apart; in recent years, issues of gay clergy, divorced clergy, women's ordination and radical services have all resulted in criticism.

POINTS OF EVALUATION

The effects of increased choice
Berger presents a strong case to show how the processes of pluralisation and secularisation are linked. The more choices a person has, the less is the support for any one organisation; 'Religion no longer legitimates the world'. The outcome is that some religious groups play the game of free religious enterprise, come to terms with the plausibility problem and try to meet the new demands and needs of their potential customers. Others may refuse to seek such accommodation with the world and develop structures which make them more private and secretive, appealing only to the highly committed.

The power of private beliefs
While the level of objective religiosity can be measured, problems must arise in assessing the significance and extent of 'private' or subjective religious activity. Religious beliefs may have some impact on a person's private behaviour even if they do not attend a church.

Extent of 'subterranean beliefs'
There is the problem of explaining the power of superstitious beliefs. Those opposed to the secularisation thesis claim that superstitions are evidence of latent religious attitudes.

Belief in the golden age of religion
There is the implication that there was a golden age of religion, when the plausibility structures were secure, and religion was a binding influence on everyone's life. Peter Worsley has even questioned whether people in primitive societies were as in awe of religion and magic as is often assumed.

THE EFFECTS OF SECULARISATION

Berger notes how different groups within societies have been affected by the processes of secularisation. He suggests its impact has been stronger

- on men than on women
- on people in the middle age range than on the very young and the old
- in cities than in the country
- on those more connected with industrial production than those in service occupations
- on Protestants and Jews than on Roman Catholics.

Research suggests that church-based religiosity is strongest in European societies among those in more marginal social situations (people left behind in the move for upward mobility; ethnic minorities; people facing various social problems). This is because the original source of secularisation was in the industrial economic sphere, in which the impact varied between social strata. The closer people were to the production process, the stronger the impact of secular values. The situation appears to be different in America (where there is a separation of Church from State), where membership of a church serves important sources of identity for all social groups.

Activity

1   Describe in your own words the trends indicated by the information in tables 12 and 13, showing adult church attendance in Britain.
2   Examine table 15 on p 101. How does the information from the table support the idea that the UK is becoming a secular society?

ARGUMENTS AGAINST THE SECULARISATION THESIS

Some sociologists argue that religion serves important human needs and so cannot be in terminal decline. Also, there are secular alternatives to religion which satisfy these needs such as nationalism, membership of political parties, or even the activities of a football fan. However, there is evidence that belief in the mystical remains significant even in a highly technological age, for a comparatively large number of people. This has led to a re-examination of the secularisation thesis.

David Martin strongly opposes the secularisation thesis. He does not dispute the view that a decline in religious observance and practice occurred after the Second World War. But he questions whether there has ever been a 'golden age of religion', when it was valued by everyone and when it influenced every aspect of their lives. Martin, like Shiner, is critical of the term 'secularisation'. He suggests that it is impossible to develop criteria to distinguish between the religious and the secular, and argues that the term has been used as a 'tool of counter-religious ideologies' to highlight the decline of religion in society and undermine its significance. Larry Shiner (see p 87) has pointed out how the term is used in many misleading ways by commentators.

THE PROBLEM OF MEASURING DECLINE

The loss of religious belief and values is hard to establish. Yet, if secularisation is occurring then it must be open to measurement. The statistics relating to membership and attendance are unreliable. Grace Davie makes the point that 'religious statistics are notoriously hard to handle'. Reliability, validity, collection and interpretation depend on many factors. Phenomenologists and interpretivists point out that statistics have to be gathered by people throughout the country, for some purpose. How they are interpreted is also open to criticism. It is their argument that statistics are misleading because:

1 Definitions of religion vary between sociologists. Therefore, different questions will be asked to measure religiosity. Also, membership figures are unreliable because different churches, denominations and other religious groups have different ways of defining it. Demerath and Hammond suggest that 'we should avoid the quick assumption that church members are always highly religious in their personal beliefs and activities, or that church non-members are otherwise irreligious'.

2 Numbers attending church weekly may be low, but numbers attending a few times in the year (Easter, Christmas or an occasional visit) are very high. Church statistics may be distorted by those who produce them; inaccuracies may result.

3 Glasner points to the problem that comparative data collected from past records may be unreliable, because different values were attached to Sunday attendance. It is inappropriate to assume that in the past people were more religious than they are today.

4 Thomas agrees that there is not enough evidence about religious patterns of behaviour in the distant past to know whether decline has occurred or if it has been consistent in every area.

5 Statistical evidence for secularisation also varies between countries. Table 14 shows that worldwide figures indicate that major world religions maintain high levels of support. There has been a rise of religious fundamentalism in many Muslim countries; Christian fundamentalism in the west has always been successful in maintaining and increasing its support.

6 The work of Herberg and others shows that there is strong evidence that attendance and membership rates are much higher in the USA. Bruce,

however, argues that the evidence for the USA may have been misinterpreted. The relative popularity of religion resulted from two factors: America's late industrialisation compared with Britain, and the significance of religion in America as a source of ethnic identity.

Tabie 14: *Estimated membership of world religions, 1990*						
CHRISTIANS	MUSLIMS	HINDUS	SIKHS	JEWS	BAHA'IS	PARSEES
1,400m	800m	580m	25m	3m	6m	9m

SOURCE: *SOCIOLOGY REVIEW* 1992

Study point
Why are religious statistics 'notoriously hard to handle'?

THE STRENGTH OF PRIVATE BELIEFS

1 The church membership and attendance statistics do not show how many people have privately held religious beliefs but are not formally registered as church members. Davie calls this 'believing without belonging'.
2 Table 15 shows the strength of private beliefs in 1991.

Table 15: *The strength of beliefs (1991)*	
BELIEFS	PERCENTAGE
Belief in God	52
Life after death	27
Belief in heaven	46
Belief in miracles	24

SOURCE: BRITISH ATTITUDE SURVEY 1991

THE IMPACT OF RELIGION IN THE MEDIA

Bradley notes that religious programmes are listened to or watched by nearly 60 per cent of the population. Every week between seven and eight million people tune into the BBC's *Songs of Praise*, and research suggests that they are not the same eight million who attend a place of worship every week.

THE IMPACT OF RELIGION ON NATIONAL LIFE IN BRITAIN

The Church still remains important as a national institution; the extent of disengagement has been over emphasised.

- The Houses of Parliament begins each day with prayers.
- Church of England Bishops have seats in the House of Lords (the 'Lords Spiritual') and play an influential role in promoting or combating legislation on a range of both religious and secular issues.
- The monarch is crowned by the Archbishop of Canterbury, is Head of the Church of England, Wales, Scotland and Northern Ireland, and 'Defender of the Faith'.
- The clergy may have lost much of their status but the quality of their education and training is better. They are better trained and vocationally oriented (in the Victorian period, the second son of a well to do family was often expected to become a clergyman).
- The Church of England remains extremely wealthy; it controls funds exceeding three billion pounds, owns estates and has other wealth producing investments.
- Religious services are held for special events including many civic rituals (eg, a coronation), and daily religious assemblies have been legal requirements in British schools.
- Members of the clergy provoke useful national debate and discussion on issues such as abortion, homosexuality, poverty and racism; eg, publications such as *The Church and the Bomb* (1982), *Faith in the City* (1985). In doing so they bring issues to wider attention and may put pressure on governments for change. Religious groups can still act as powerful pressure groups, influencing those in positions of power in society. For example, LIFE and SPUC (The Society for the Protection of the Unborn Child) are mainly Catholic organisations seeking to make abortion completely illegal. In Northern Ireland, religious organisations continue to have a significant input into social and political life.
- The emergence of religious political groups such as the Christian New Right in America (Evangelical Protestantism) has been a powerful influence on political values (especially those of the Republican Party). Its aims have been to develop strong support for a return to traditional values, and form the basis for a new sense of moral regeneration. The Promise Keepers would be an example of this movement (see p 53).
- For Martin, disengagement would not be something to oppose, as the Church's specialisation in theological matters may result in a purer form of religion, uncontaminated by secular concerns such as political and economic issues. Like Durkheim, he sees religion as an important source of moral order in society and its decline could lead to social breakdown and the development of totalitarian leaders.

⬤

Why is Martin critical of the term 'secularisation', although he accepts that changes have occurred leaving the churches with fewer members?

THE SACRED RETAINS SIGNIFICANCE

• Society has not become completely desacrilised. Although science has contributed to our understanding, it has not replaced religious beliefs, or those in the supernatural, or the mystical.
• While science explains birth and death in terms of physiological and biological factors, religion explains the 'ultimate meanings' of these events.
• Religious rituals remain important in rites of passage which are still widely used.
• Greeley sees the growth and development of new religious movements as a process of 'resacrilisation' – the interest and belief in the sacred is being re-established. The increase in religious options may make the idea of an established Church outdated, but development of world faiths in Britain (see p 101) show how important they are. Their values and powers for people cannot be dismissed.

RELIGIOUS VALUES REMAIN STRONG

• Even people who say they are not religious, sometimes have a strong sense of the mystical. Martin has pointed out that between 20–45 per cent of people express beliefs in subterranean theologies (see table 2a, p 15).
• Also, there are many new religious movements emerging which refute this (see p 74). They represent a transformation of religion rather than decline.
• The nature of religious practice and commitment may have changed. Members of new religious movements are more committed and have stronger or purer religious beliefs than members of established churches.
• Those who see decline have misunderstood the nature of statistical data; they have underestimated the significance of religion in a private sense in people's lives; and they fail to understand the nature of social change and the processes of globalisation, which is transforming religion into hitherto unknown systems. The scientific approach to life is losing its attractions, whereas the mystical is gaining support. New Age movements represent a spiritual quest by people in postmodern society.

Study point

Suggest how the outcomes of religious attitude and belief surveys might be interpreted by Wilson and Martin.

RELIGION IS NOT IRRELEVANT

Rodney Stark and William Bainbridge argue that religion continues to satisfy important social needs in every society. Religion will always be a relevant force fulfilling human needs, but not necessarily in the traditional structures. It will operate at different levels, driving people into new ways of acting and responding to the world to gain understanding and knowledge about their place in it. These writers emphasise the significance of religion for cultural defence and transition.

Cultural defence

Where a people have a common religion and are threatened by another internal or external force of a different religion or secular ideology, the religious institutions can be seen as defenders of the people and their culture. In Northern Ireland, the Catholic Church has defended the rights and interests of the minority population; the Protestant Churches have defended the interests of the Unionists.

Cultural transition

Religion can help an immigrant population come to terms with problems of migration and the major cultural transition they face. Religion can help bind them together, provide them with a means of coping with hostility and give them a sense of self-worth; it can help them to learn the new language and to adjust to their new circumstances. The result is that religious groups appear to vary in their levels of decline and their growth. For example, some of the most conservative Protestant sects (fundamentalists, Presbyterians, evangelicals, pentacostalists) have retained strong support (especially in societies under some kind of threat), and in some cases they have gained in strength. They have been especially effective in retaining the support of children and young people, which is not the case with the mainstream orthodox churches.

THE GROWTH OF PRIVATE WORSHIP

Individuation

Robert Bellah argues that it is wrong to claim that because there has been a fall in attendances in places of public worship, that religion is therefore in decline. In fact, people have become more able to adopt private form of spiritual quest. They pick and choose and select from a wide range of choices. This he describes as a process of individuation. It means that many people are devout without necessarily being members of any particular religious organisation. However, critics of Bellah would ask how it is possible to know the extent of individuation among those who adopt private religious practices. Some form of measure would be required to confirm this viewpoint.

Invisible religion

Thomas Luckmann argues that there are major changes underway in religious systems and values. Where it has been the traditional stance of religion to provide people with highly structured institutions and to give answers to other-worldly matters, the emphasis has moved to issues of individual self-development, and freedoms for personal self-expression and morality. He suggests that in the future, religion will inform a new social consciousness in which people will look for those values, organisations and contacts which make most sense to them. There will be a loss of institutionalised religion, but a growth in the privatised forms of belief systems together with concerns for individualism. This search for self-actualisation, is driven by a religious impulse. People need to make sense of their lives and their world, and do so by constructing a sacred cosmos (see also p 43).

He describes this process as the effects of 'invisible religion'. As society undergoes change and development so the traditional religious systems will alter and new forms will emerge. There is, therefore, no decline in religion; merely constant change. For Timothy Crippen it is the nation state which 'represents the most dominant, extensive and inclusive boundary of moral identity in modern societies ... it is the dominant form of religious consciousness.' This represents the transformation of the old sacred symbols into the new.

Study point
1 Consider the problems associated with Bellah's view in assessing the extent of individuation.
2 What problems might a researcher have in assessing the numbers of people who hold private religious beliefs and values?
3 Discuss the implication of Luckmann's view, that even consumerism, the drive for more material goods, status and prestige, is the manifestation of the new 'invisible religion'.

EVALUATION

- Eldridge has pointed out that although Martin and Wilson are seen as disputants concerning the nature and significance of secularisation, they actually share a similar fear. This is 'the problem of order for a society, engendered by the absence of reliable authority and secure knowledge'. Martin is hopeful that man's religious impulse is merely taking a series of diversions, and will eventually return to more orthodox positions in the search for understanding about the ultimate issues of life. Wilson seems fearful that in modern (and postmodern) society, people increasingly lack a unifying sense of moral order to give stability to society. He looks back to a world, now lost, in which this once existed. His solutions are described by Eldridge as 'an interpretation resulting in conservative nihilism.'

- There is always a problem in knowing whether those who dispute the processes of secularisation and see the value of religion in the process of cultural defence and transition, have some vested interest in presenting their arguments. Martin is himself an ordained Anglican priest.

SUMMARY

There is a considerable debate in sociology about whether or not religion is in decline. Some sociologists argue that while it may seem common sense to point to a loss of the influence of religion in people's lives, much hinges on definitions of religious activity. Some have questioned the idea of secularisation and suggested that it is ideological. It is part of contemporary cultural wisdom; it seems to explain the world as we see it, yet lacks comprehensive evidence to support it. From a postmodernist perspective, secularisation is an outmoded concept; it no longer provides insights about the meaning of religion in a pluralistic and fragmented society. The outcome is the lucky dip approach in which those who wish to can select from the wide range of options and discard them if they wish to. On this view there is no single concept which is sufficient to explain this.

From the perspective of the orthodox churches in Britain, a limited version of the concept of secularisation does make sense. This enables researchers to examine variations between contemporary societies, in levels and strength of beliefs and attitudes towards spiritual matters at a national and personal level (especially in the fields of superstition, magic, cults and associated mysterious belief systems which have no organised structure or membership). It is always useful to be aware of the problems pointed out by Shiner in examining how the concept is used and its implications.

STUDY ⓢ GUIDES

Group work

Hold a debate. The following motion can be used:

'This house believes that religious thinking, practices and institutions have declined in social significance'.

Key Concepts Activity

Choose the correct definition for the following key concepts. Write the definitions on Key Concept Cards for revision purposes (see p 3).

1 Religiosity
2 Dechristianisation
3 Desacrilisation
4 Rationalisation
5 Laicisation
6 Individuation
7 Structural differentiation
8 Areligiosity
9 Disengagement
10 Disenchantment

a The historical process whereby social structures become increasingly specialised and segregated.

b The state of being without religious belief and thus without religious practices.

c The process by which the State and the Church become increasingly separate and distinct entities, with a corresponding loss of power and influence of the Church over the State.

d A decline in belief in the sacred.

e The process whereby religious institutions become less important in the individual's search for meaning.

f A process described by Weber in which, as a result of the development of science and rational modes of thought, the explanations of natural phenomena provided by beliefs in magic, miracles and the supernatural are displaced.

g The process whereby modern western societies are turning away from Christianity, towards secular existence, non-standard Christian-inspired cults or non-Christian religions.

h The sense of the religious in the individual.

i The process whereby modern societies increasingly use rationality to address and solve problems.

j The movement from a Christian era to a secular age.

Practice questions

1 'Religious thinking, practices and institutions have declined in social significance'. Evaluate sociological arguments and evidence both for and against this view.

2 a Briefly outline what sociologists mean by the term 'secularisation'.
  b Outline three problems faced by sociologists in attempting to measure secularisation.
  c Identify and discuss three criticisms of the secularisation thesis.
  d Critically discuss the evidence for the secularisation of Britain.
3 Does the emergence of new religious movements challenge the secularisation thesis?

Coursework suggestions

Conduct a study on secularisation in your local area. Decide on the definition of secularisation which you will adopt, and justify its use.

- Use secondary sources such as church attendance and membership, and the increase or decrease in the number of churches, chapels or other places of religious meeting. Also, obtain statistics to show numbers in the area being studied who attend football matches, the cinemas, the theatres or other places of public meeting.
- Include some observational material based on numbers attending a sample of places of worship.
- Examine and analyse your data in terms of your definition of secularisation.
- Consider the views of the critics of the term. Reach some conclusions based on your findings.

7

THE ETHNIC RELIGIONS IN MULTI-CULTURAL BRITAIN

Introduction

THIS CHAPTER EXAMINES the religions of some of the ethnic groups who make up the multi-cultural society of modern Britain to see the functions they serve, their meaning for members and their implications for the analysis of religious change in Britain.

Table 16: *Theorists, concepts and issues in this chapter*		
KEY THEORISTS AND AUTHORS	KEY CONCEPTS	KEY ISSUES
Marx: Conflict theory	Discrimination Exploitation	The religious organisations of ethnic minority groups in multi cultural Britain; in particular:
Durkheim: Functionalism	Social solidarity	• Afro-Caribbeans: Pentacostalism and Rastafarianism • The Jews: Judaism
Weber: Action theory	Social change Ethnic groups	• Muslims: Islam
Berger & Luckmann Phenomenology	Universe of meaning	• Sikhs: Sikhism • Hindus: Hinduism
Postmodernist views Grace Davie	Fragmentation Fundamentalism	The strengths of these religions Their functions for members Their significance in modern society

MULTI-CULTURALISM AND ETHNIC GROUPS

In describing Britain as a multi-cultural society, sociologists are drawing attention to the fact that there are many different patterns of social life which relate to the various communities who inhabit it. A culture describes all those ways of behaving which include languages, dress, religious and other beliefs, diet and leisure interests. It also includes all those socially inherited patterns of life with which people identify and which are passed on from generation to generation. Cultural norms arise (including religious ones) in relation to these, and shape the ways in which people behave. People then come to feel that these ways of proceeding are the correct ways; they make sense of them and they are satisfying emotionally and intellectually.

Weber described **ethnic groups** as 'human groups which cherish a belief in their common origins of such a kind that it provides a basis for the creation of a community'. Their members share cultural characteristics which are different in some respects to those of the majority population. They may have a sense of common origin, especially where there is a shared language or religion. While some groups have become assimilated so that they are hard to identify (many Jewish people arriving at the turn of the century have lost their Jewish identity), other groups remain identifiable through their cultural activities. Many of these have enriched the culture of the host society, by introducing new foods (eg, in 1997 a survey indicated that British people now eat 205 million poppadoms every year), fashions, drama, music, and many other social features, often taken for granted.

THE RECENT ORIGIN OF MINORITY GROUPS IN BRITAIN

Although there have been many black and other minority groups in Britain since recorded history, in the nineteenth century there was a large immigration of Jews from mainland Europe seeking to escape persecution, especially from Russia; there was also large scale immigration from Ireland, escaping famine; and in the early twentieth century, immigrants arrived from Africa, the Caribbean, China and parts of Europe. Some came as members of the armed forces during the Second World War. Levels of immigration from the new Commonwealth (India, Pakistan, Bangladesh, the Caribbean) increased thereafter.

There was also major demand for labour as Britain rebuilt its postwar economy, which immigrants provided, often filling the least attractive jobs. Naturally, they also brought with them their own religious customs. The religions of ethnic minorities are interesting to sociologists both because they are intrinsically significant to social life and because they provide a source of comparison for the ways in which religion functions and has meaning in wider British society.

THE RESPONSE OF CHRISTIAN CHURCHES

The arrival of increasing numbers of ethnic minority groups, (especially those with a background familiarity with Christianity) provided mainstream Christian churches with the potential for growth, by encouraging new immigrants to become members of their congregations. For the most part they failed to do so, and smaller, more independent churches and denominations developed, although the effect may have been to enrich the religious opportunities within inner city areas. Not unsurprisingly, those from non-Christian backgrounds preferred to establish their own temples, mosques and other places of worship. The differences in patterns of membership over time can be seen in table 17.

Table 17: *UK membership of non-Christian religions (millions)*			
UK NON-TRINITARIAN RELIGIONS	1975	1990	1995
Muslims	0.41	0.99	1.11
Sikhs	0.12	0.39	0.62
Hindus	0.11	0.14	0.15
Jews	0.12	0.12	0.12

NOTE: NON-TRINITARIAN RELIGIONS ARE THOSE THAT DO NOT BELIEVE IN THE UNITY OF THE TRINITY IN ONE GOD

SOURCE: *SOCIAL TRENDS* (1997)

Study point

Draw out some implications from table 17 with regard to the differences in religious observance. How does the data challenge the idea that Britain is becoming a more secular society?

The dominant ethnic minority religions in Britain are those of Judaism; the Afro-Caribbeans; the Hindus; Muslims and the Sikhs. Each one retains strong support from their comparatively small populations.

JUDAISM

The word Jew means a member of the tribe of Judah, the royal tribe of David. Judaism dates from about 8th century BC. Hebrew history is recorded in the Bible, and the Old Testament provides details of the cultural heritage of the Jews in western civilisation. Exodus describes how the Jews were led by Moses from slavery in search of the promised land. In the course of this quest the Jews suffered persecution, and communities appeared in many areas of the world, each retaining its cultural roots as a source of identity. Belief in the ideal of success was encouraged by the rabbinical tradition, which encouraged members to attain the highest levels of excellence in whatever they undertook. As a successful minority group, producing many eminent merchants, traders, academics, actors and business people, they frequently became scapegoats for the economic or other social problems which arose in the areas in which they lived.

In the 1880s, there was mass migration from Israel to USA, when about two million Jews fled there. In 1948, the state of Israel was established to provide a homeland for Jews; it is estimated that there are Jews in Israel from over 100 different cultural backgrounds. In the 1990s there were approximately five million Jews in USA, about the same as in Israel. There were about 300,000 practising Jews in Britain.

THE LIBERAL JEWISH SYNAGOGUE HAS ABOUT 15,000 MEMBERS IN THE UK. THEIR AIM IS TO MAKE THE JEWISH RELIGION MORE APPROPRIATE TO A MODERN AGE. SUGGEST WHY CRITICS BELIEVE THAT THIS WILL UNDERMINE ITS STRENGTH

The Jewish population is divided between those who have become assimilated into the population and no longer practise Judaism as a religion (an unknown number); those who think that they should retain all their traditions in a strict way (perhaps as many as 80 per cent), and those who maintain some limited features of belief and practice, but who accept patterns of reform (the remaining 20 per cent).

Those who acknowledge their roots most fervently tend to cluster in certain areas of cities; this is because they can obtain the foods they require, visit synagogues and maintain a sense of cultural identity through their social contacts. They favour continuity, support their protective institutions and obey strict rules of living in accordance with the Talmud (the primary source of Jewish religious law). Surveys suggest that as many as 33 per cent of orthodox Jews attend Synagogue at least once a week.

The less strict group acknowledges the need for change and adaptation for the future. They are more outward-looking, and recommend ways of making it easier for members to follow the religious rules of Judaism (some of which are very demanding). Judaism is a religion which includes many taboos in relation to food and other aspects of life, defined as sacred to maintain purity. The most orthodox Jews have traditionally maintained strict social boundaries, so that marriage with non-Jewish people is forbidden.

POINTS OF SOCIOLOGICAL SIGNIFICANCE

- The Jews in Britain are more likely to be religiously observant than the members of major British Christian churches.
- The success of Jewish people in work can be attributed to the 'rabbinical tradition' in which the religious teachers (rabbis) who are skilled interpreters of the Torah, teach correct behaviour and encourage a spirit of excellence in everyday life.
- The Jews face a similar problem to many other religious groups, as to whether or not they should become more insular to protect their heritage, or turn outwards and allow reforms which make it easier to retain traditions which might otherwise be lost. In Israel, because there are many threats facing the Jewish population, orthodox Jews became more dominant in political life during the 1990s. In Britain, the fear may be that intermarriages will undermine the Jewish identity of future generations.
- Judaism provides its members with a strong sense of identity and with clear ideals and codes of morality.
- Because Judaism is not a convertionist religion, there has been decline in the number of practising Jews in Britain, from about 400,000 in the 1950s to about 300,000 in the 1990s. The decline is also due to increased levels of migration to Israel.

- The Jewish population in Britain is an ageing one, as family size is reduced (in common with the rest of the population) and remains concentrated in the major cities.
- There has been an increase in regional variations between the strength and significance of both mainstream Christianity and ethnic religious movements.

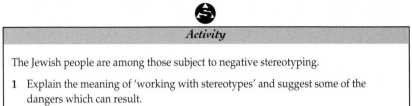

Activity

The Jewish people are among those subject to negative stereotyping.

1 Explain the meaning of 'working with stereotypes' and suggest some of the dangers which can result.
2 Consider why some people with a Jewish background wished to become assimilated into British society, while others wished to emphasise their Jewishness and become more insular.

RELIGIONS OF AFRO-CARIBBEANS

There are about 500,000 people in Britain with roots in the Caribbean. Many have lived in Britain for many generations, and a high proportion have arrived since the Second World War. Of those who are religious, about 20 per cent are members of Christian churches; but the highest proportion, perhaps 70 per cent, are involved with the Pentecostalists. Grace Davie suggests that in 1990, membership of Afro-Caribbean churches was about 70,000:

> *'grouped into 965 congregations, which have in difficult circumstances become an important hub of effective community life. They represent an impressive undertaking.'*
>
> *Religion in Britain since 1945 (1996)*

There are also about 150,000 people from Africa, who also turn to various black-led churches.

RELIGIOUS ATTACHMENT

David Pearson described how West Indians have become more attached to religious organisations than almost any other formal association.

- Although levels of membership and participation in Britain are high compared to the white population, they are lower than in the Caribbean.

- Choice of organisation was determined to some extent by their perception of the mainstream British churches as dull and tedious, whereas they preferred a more spontaneous and lively service; it was also influenced by their reception among white congregations, which was often hostile.
- This reflects the experiences which many first generation immigrants encountered on first arriving in Britain. For some, the effects of alienation, prejudice and discrimination served to increase the need for a sense of community and to find secure organisations which offered hope for a better future.

RELIGIOUS ATTITUDES

Pearson found generational differences.

- Many younger West Indians (especially second generation) were found to be influenced by the irreligious attitudes of their white peers, a process reinforced by a loosening of controls within West Indian households and communities. Consequently, there was found to be a decline in attendance and membership among this sector.
- There appeared to be a process of secularisation within the Afro-Caribbeans community also. As Pearson points out, this can be attributed to an amalgam of both past and present influences.
- The main exception to the secularisation process among Afro-Caribbeans is the growth of sectarian membership, especially among Pentecostal movements and also among some sects with predominantly white membership, such as Seventh Day Adventists and Jehovah's Witnesses.
- Although the West Indian Church membership is small, it is higher than in the mainstream Christian churches. The members of these sects do not regard black members in a negative way, perhaps because they already perceive themselves as outsiders to the orthodox religious world and have more sympathy for others who wish to join them. These sects also provide a more informal structure and type of worship.

THE PENTACOSTAL ORGANISATIONS

Many of the Pentecostal churches are of recent foundation, some appearing in the 1960s and 1970s, such as The New Testament Church of God. Their formation coincided with an increase in racial hostility. The attractions of these churches are that the services do not require high levels of verbal fluency for membership; they are family centred and have a level of entertainment with singing and dancing which makes them enjoyable.

⬥

Study point

In 1997, a Bristol based Gospel singer was fined £100 after neighbours complained about late night chanting and clapping sessions; the Pastor of the Christian fellowship in North London was fined £200 for the volume of its singing. They complained that they were being prosecuted for being successful in attracting huge congregations. Do you think mainstream churches should try to compete by enlivening their services?

Membership

This depends only on the acceptance of the organisations' doctrines and the agreement to live accordingly. Members may be encouraged to lead exemplary lives, and forbidden to take part in a more secular lifestyle. For Afro-Caribbeans, membership of a Pentecostal church may have advantages in that they attain higher status as a result of their membership by other believers; but there may be disadvantages in membership:

- They are open to criticism from black non-members, who may feel that their religious behaviour presents a negative image of West Indian ways of life.
- They may be viewed as deviant and puritanical.
- Members of the white community may see them as exclusive, leading secluded lives and indulging in unusual religious rituals which involve music and colourful clothes. Church members could be in danger of becoming isolated from other black people and the white population.

RASTAFARIANISM

Rastafarianism became a popular movement for younger West Indians in the 1970s and 80s. It developed in the Caribbean, where Marcus Garvey thought that West Indians were a lost tribe of Israel who had been enslaved by whites and taken to the West Indies. The way for black people to achieve success and escape poverty, was to recognise the biblical evidence that Haile Selassie, Emperor of Ethiopia since 1930 when he was known as Ras (Prince) Tafari was the true Messiah living in their place of origin.

In 1982 a plea was made (and subsequently accepted) for Rastafarianism to be recognised as a valid religion and for members to be allowed to enjoy full religious rights. The Catholic Commission for Racial Justice urged that Rastafarian style of dress, including dreadlock hairstyle, should be accepted by society as authentic religious expressions and legitimate cultural forms. It was argued that many of the symbols and mythology of the movement could be accounted for as a positive response to the West Indian community's historical experience of enslavement, transportation, poverty, immigration and racial hostility by whites. The demand was to recognise that Rastafarianism represented something positive and important to British society.

POINTS OF SOCIOLOGICAL SIGNIFICANCE

Community

For black congregations, the sense of community grows from the Church. However, the Church of England was traditionally a part of the existing, white community.

Deprivation

The churches to which Afro-Caribbeans turn tend to give support and spiritual help to those who suffer deprivation. Pentacostalism has traditionally appealed to a working class congregation.

Racism

Membership of such churches may not, therefore, be simply an extension of the way they observed religion in the West Indies, but more a response to racialism.

Social stratification

Pearson concluded that these religious groups represented expressions of social discontent. The different churches to which they turned (whether Anglican, Catholic or Pentacostal) represented subtle divisions between West Indian groups. These reinforced status distinctions between them. The upwardly mobile Afro-Caribbeans were attached to the more traditional churches, whereas the lower class West Indians were likely to become attached to religiously separate Pentecostal churches.

Gender

Some studies have shown that male membership of Pentecostal churches is greater than female membership, which may be accounted for by the fact that Afro-Caribbean men feel greater loss of status in Britain than women.

Compensation

Stark and Bainbridge have argued that religion can act as compensation, meeting the complex needs of individuals by providing various kinds of rewards; this is particularly relevant to this ethnic group, which is 30 per cent more likely to suffer poverty and ill health than the non-black population (Policy Studies Institute, 1997).

Activity

Discuss ways of testing the hypothesis that mainstream churches have more middle class members than ethnic minority sects. What kinds of problems might be encountered in gathering the data?

MUSLIMS

Muslim beliefs and practices involve acceptance of the prophet Mohammed as God's special messenger, undertaking frequent pilgrimages to the Holy City of Mecca, and observing Holy Days and rituals absolutely. Orthodox Muslims turn to Mecca and pray to Allah five times a day, abstain from pork and alcohol, and fast during the holy period of Ramadan. The revelations of Mohammed are revealed in the Koran which consists of 114 chapters. Islam means submission; those who submit to the teachings are called Muslims.

WHAT FUNCTION DOES ISLAM SERVE FOR MUSLIMS WHO SETTLE IN THE UK FROM VARIOUS PARTS OF THE WORLD?

Muslims form the largest non-Christian minority in Britain. In the 1990s, there were approximately one million members of the Muslim (Islamic) community, although not all practise their religions of origin. The largest proportion originate from Pakistan and Bangladesh. This group has also suffered high levels of prejudice and discrimination while settling in Britain, in every sphere of social life. British Muslims are a young population, having a high proportion of their numbers in the age range 18–44 years. In the indigenous British population, this age group is generally irreligious.

In some countries, especially the Middle East, Muslim governments have been established consisting largely of Muslim clergy. It is their intention to reveal the true religion to the mass of people and establish a Muslim State based on religious principles. Like most other ethnic groups, Muslims in Britain are also divided into a variety of religious traditions which are defined by their political and ethnic background. Most British Muslims are Sunnis, and the remainder Shias. The two groups have developed many differences in their practices and have many sects. In some areas of the world (notably Pakistan), they are hostile to each other.

Feminists have argued that in Islam, women are relegated to a secondary role and denied career opportunities. However, others have suggested that the society of Islam safeguards women from denigration, holds them in high regard, and allocates them roles different to those of men, but of equal status. While women in Islamic societies wear purdah (a veil) regarded by some as a mark of oppression, supporters of Islam suggest that in western societies the equivalent is the make-up which masks women's faces.

Study point

Why do you think the 16–24 age group are more irreligious than those aged 25–45? Discuss ways of researching this hypothesis.

POINTS OF SOCIOLOGICAL SIGNIFICANCE

- There are several factors which inhibit a shared sense of Muslim identity: different Muslim groups hold different attitudes to their life in UK. For some it is a temporary religious phase; for others it is permanent; members vary in their degree of commitment to traditional Muslim values.
- Since 1986, Muslims have outnumbered the combined membership of Methodists and Baptists in Britain.
- There has been a steady increase in the number of mosques in Britain, from 4 in 1964, to 320 in 1995.
- More women attend mosques in Britain than in traditional Muslim countries. This is because the mosque is a focus of social life. It is a place where they can meet friends, share problems and feel a greater sense of community.
- In Britain, Muslim women have low rates of economic activity. This may result among an older generation from their frequently poor standard of English, from the cultural value of purdah (seclusion), and from the fact that they came to Britain mainly as dependants and not as workers.
- A report in 1997 suggested that practising Muslims in Britain could outnumber practising Anglicans by the year 2002.

HINDUS

Hindu means 'India', and Hinduism is considered to be the oldest living religion, possibly founded more than 4,000 years ago. It is polytheistic (having many gods), although it incorporates the concept of a supreme spirit, Brahman, of which all living things are a part. Some of the gods are localised and some have special significance.

For Hindus, life is a circular and unending journey. Hinduism involves a belief in cycles of reincarnation, a moral law, mystical contemplation, special diet and self-denying practices. These are set out in the sacred books, the Vedas, the Brahmans and the Upanishads, and also in epic poems (these teach concepts and rules of morality; among the most famous is The Bhaghavad-Gita). The religion also has sacred men called gurus, who teach its ideals.

As in Christian religion, there are numerous sects of Hinduism, each involving great differences in doctrine and ritual within the framework of a caste structure. The castes represent four classes of early Hindu society. These are the Brahmins (priests), the Kshatriayas (the warriors), the Vaisyas (the traders) and the Shudras (the servants and labourers); below them are the 'untouchables'. Caste membership traditionally determines every aspect of social life: where a person lives, what they can eat, what occupation they can undertake and whom they can marry. A report by Dilip Hiro examined the plight of 80 million untouchables in India, and urged the undermining of the whole caste system by attacking the tradition of the hereditary priesthood, and supplanting it with a rational system of properly trained priests in public institutions open to all Hindus, including the untouchables.

Study point
Suggest some similarities and differences between caste and class.

Inevitably, it is difficult for Hindus to practise their traditional devotions in Britain in the way they might in India. Traditionally, great reverence is paid to the Brahmin teachers, and devout Hindus visit them frequently to hear scriptures being recited. But private rituals can be conducted in the home, by having special shrines or images of a deity, and lighting incense sticks, or in communal temples. These are important as community centres, for festival celebrations and for teaching purposes.

There are about 400,000 Hindus in the British population, although not all are practising. While many are long standing members of British society, most have their roots in various parts of the Indian subcontinent. Like all religions, Hinduism advocates certain ideals for its members which influence daily behaviour. Members may not necessarily attain each one. The first is the ideal of obedience to the teacher; the second is that of the good householder and married person; the third is a period of quiet reflection or retreat from the outside world; and the fourth is that of the complete ascetic life, living in spiritual isolation from the world, like a hermit or beggar. This leads to the significance of pilgrimage for the Hindu, to gain spiritual merit.

HINDUS HAVE THREE PRINCIPAL GODS; THE GOD SHIVA HAS MANY HANDS. WHY DO RELIGIONS MAKE USE OF SUCH SYMBOLS IN THEIR WORSHIP?

POINTS OF SOCIOLOGICAL SIGNIFICANCE

- Hindu-influenced sects in British society include the International Society for Krishna Consciousness, and The Hare Krishna Movement.
- The number of Hindu temples in Britain has increased to about 130 since 1963.
- Hindus are divided by caste, language and cultural background. Many castes have their own deities and rituals. The means of admission to Hinduism is to be incorporated as a member of a caste. Once admitted, a person has a certain leeway in the beliefs they hold. In this respect it is not unlike the Christian who holds some religious, some superstitious and some pagan beliefs within their overall ideology of the world.

- Hinduism emphasises the significance of women in relation to the family and the care of children, and they have special deities.

Beliefs

- Hinduism has proved capable of absorbing new values and new doctrines, adopting the ideals of social service from Christian missions to India and developing new forms of religion for their members.
- It has also encouraged members to accept that all religions are good and all provide ways to one final divine goal. Tolerance remains an important ideal for Hindus.

Appeal of Hinduism

Of all the Eastern religions, aspects of Hinduism appear to have had the greatest appeal for people in the west:

- Prince Charles has a guru, an Indian doctor who advocates homeopathy, as does the Queen.
- The author Christopher Isherwood wrote a book in 1939, entitled *My Guru and His Disciples*.
- Aldous Huxley admired Hinduism and its philosophy.
- In the 1960s, The Beatles discovered the Maharishi, and made use of the Indian sitar in some of their music.
- In the 1970s, the Hare Krishna movement became popular, with a strict regime of celibacy and chanting.
- In the 1990s the New Age and Mind-Body-Spirit festivals offer spiritual opportunities.
- Many eminent people practise TM (Transcendental Meditation); closely associated with TM is Yoga, a well known system of relaxation.

Activity
Investigate the extent to which Yoga and TM have lost their association with Hindu practices in Britain among practitioners.

SIKHS

The home of Sikhism is the Punjab area of northern India. This was a sovereign nation before being divided between India and Pakistan in 1947. The largest migration of Sikh males to Britain was shortly after 1947, followed in the 1960s by women and children. Sikhs arrived in Britain often with a good command of English and sharing the values of educational success and business enterprise.

The majority appeared to have a view of long-term migration, while retaining their cultural values. Full integration to western society was not part of the agenda, although tolerance and mutual respect was. Consequently, Sikhs have been among the more economically successful of the ethnic minority groups in Britain. Sikh women also play important roles in the economy and within the household, although sex roles are generally clearly demarcated, and arranged marriages preferred.

In 1997 there were approximately 400,000 Sikhs in Britain. A minority of British Sikhs arrived in the 1970s from Uganda in East Africa, having been expelled by the dictator, Idi Amin. Many Sikhs also fought for Britain during the Second World War (several won the VC).

Partition was the culmination of clashes between the Muslims and Hindus, which still erupt from time to time. The Sikh Golden temple (the holiest Sikh shrine) in Amrisar (in the Punjab) was destroyed by Indian government forces in 1984; ill feeling surfaces occasionally in contemporary Britain. Pro-Sikh independence groups in India have a strong support among British Sikhs.

Their first place of worship was established in Putney in the suburbs of London, in 1911, and there are now more than 180 Sikh temples in Britain. As with Hindus, temples serve as a place of worship and somewhere in which Sikhs can meet as a community. Sikh religion is a mixture of Hindu and Muslim practices. It is a comparatively recent world religion, dating from about the middle of the 15th century, when it was founded by the guru, Nanak. His followers are Sikhs (disciples). It is a monotheistic religion which incorporates ideas from two great religious – Hinduism and Islam. The one God is known by various names: he is Allah, Rama and Krishna.

At their initiation, male Sikhs swear to observe five rules:

1   to wear turbans, and leave their hair and beards uncut
2   to wear a comb (symbolic of spirituality)
3   to wear a steel bracelet (a symbol of brotherhood)
4   to wear a knee length garment (symbolic of modesty)
5   to carry a dagger (symbolic of their belief in protecting the weak).

In 1997, Sikh leaders complained that the ban on servicemen wearing turbans in the British armed forces offended their religious principles, although Sikhs had been exempted from having to wear crash helmets on motor cycles 20 years previously. Because carrying a dagger is a punishable offence in British law (regarded as an offensive weapon), British Sikhs carry plastic daggers on their persons, thus maintaining their religious tradition but adapting to the society in which they live.

POINTS OF SOCIOLOGICAL SIGNIFICANCE

Sikhism as a source of identity

There was a strong reassertion of Sikh identity in response to prejudice and discrimination in the 1970s. While proving successful in many aspects of wider social life (in work and leisure activities), Sikhs have retained many traditional ways of life. Extended families and concern for wider kin are common values.

Beliefs

The religious belief system of the Sikhs is naturally complex, but in addition to similarities with Hinduism, the religion also shares many features in common with Christianity. Sikhs believe that there is one God, who is the creator; He is seen as personal, offering salvation to every believer who lives a good life. All Sikhs are equal in the eyes of God.

The significance of caste

- There have been some tensions between different Sikh sects, based on caste background. East African Sikhs tended to enhance their social position by emphasising religious orthodoxy and doctrinal respectability, in the face of a group who valued status respectability.
- Robert Jeffcoate and Barbara Mayor report that people from lower castes are frequently determined to take advantage of the opportunities provided by migration to discard their cultural backgrounds. Life in a class society is sometimes regarded as preferable to that of a caste system.
- Those of high caste (which determines the temple attended) may deter their children from social contact with those of inferior caste.

Activity
1 Discuss why it might be useful to know whether there is any strengthening or decline in the religious values of young Sikhs.
2 How might such findings relate to changing levels of social stability or instability between groups?

POINTS OF EVALUATION

THE GROWTH OF ETHNIC MINORITY RELIGIONS

These faiths have produced religious expansion in Britain, in an overall framework of decline in religious activity among the host population.

POSSIBLE SOURCES OF CONFLICT

Some studies have suggested that there are sources of conflict which result. Not all members of the ethnic minorities are involved in the religions of their contemporaries. Some may be hostile to those who are; religious identity is sometimes related to national identity and can lead to intercommunal conflict. In some instances, religious membership may be associated with caste membership, also preventing good wider social relations.

GENERATIONAL DIFFERENCES

- The **first** generation of ethnic minority members tended to be more lax in their religious attitudes. There were few facilities for worship, and little family or kin support to influence them in this respect.
- The **second** generation became more orthodox, enjoying family support and expectations, more opportunities for worship in customary ways and a stronger desire to learn more about their roots.
- The **third** generation who became more westernised (perhaps losing their mother tongue), may also have adopted western attitudes towards religion, which showed less interest and lower levels of attachment to religious values and institutions. They may also be in a position to examine alternatives to their own religion.

CHANGES IN THE RELIGION OF ORIGIN

Meanwhile, changes may also be occurring in the religion of origin as forces of nationalism or westernisation affect it. This may make it of stronger or weaker attraction to its British members (as in the case of Islam and Judaism, which have both become more powerful ideologies in recent years). A relative decline in racial hostility may also serve to make attachment to a religious culture less necessary.

Study point

Consider how a sociologist might undertake a research project to see if there are generational differences in religious values. What problems might be encountered in obtaining the data?

THEORIES OF ETHNIC RELIGIONS

In considering the significance of the role and impact of the religions of ethnic minorities in Britain, it is useful to consider how theorists would interpret them.

FUNCTIONALISTS

Functionalists argue that religion is an important institution for promoting **social solidarity** among communities and in society generally.

The function of social solidarity

Ethnic minorities require a strong sense of social solidarity in a new society. They can achieve this through their religious affiliations. It is not surprising therefore that all the religions of ethnic minorities show higher levels of religious involvement than among the host population.

The function of status respectability

By attending church, synagogue or temple, members may achieve social status and recognition in the community. It may also serve as a source of identity, and social and cultural protection.

The function of cultural defence

Places of worship may promote cultural values such as social interaction, teaching and learning. They may also provide the leadership with an opportunity to speak out against the patterns of intolerance or inequality which members encounter, and provide younger members with opportunities for sporting and other social activities.

The function of community and shared values

Ties of religion can be the basis of economic and political relationships. Shared religious values may be the basis on which loans are obtained, business transacted or associations formed. This is stronger among Asian ethnic minorities than Afro-Caribbean, although Pentacostalism does involve an entire lifestyle for members.

Points of criticism

- Devout membership of ethnic religious groups may also serve to isolate members. They may become detached from others in their community who are less inclined to follow tradition and may seek assimilation and integration into wider society. This conflict could serve to fragment the community.
- They may become detached from wider society. Some religious groups seek doctrinal respectability by holding strongly to very traditional values, customs and beliefs (such as orthodox Jews, fundamentalist Muslims or low caste Sikhs) which may also serve to separate them from wider society. In Israel, a powerful rabbi ruled that women who wear wigs in a synagogue should be excommunicated; orthodox Jews believe that realistic wigs are immodest. Such views may be seen as extremist and deviating from the norm of the more secular or less strongly religious way of life.

MARXISTS

Marxists would suggest that religion inhibits social change and that the use of the religion of the ethnic minorities prevents them from seeing the true cause of their problems in contemporary society.

False consciousness

Members of ethnic minority groups who encounter the most serious problems of accommodating to British society, either through **discrimination** or lack of opportunity, may turn to sect membership. This is seen by Marxist analysts as an example of **false consciousness**; they are unable to see the origins of their oppression. Their real source of comfort should be through political processes.

The power of the caste system

This operates in Hindu India and subtly reappears in Britain in both Hindu and Sikh religions. It serves to divide communities, which ought to be united against racism and disadvantage.

Points of criticism

Marxist analysis has traditionally ignored the idea that religious values could be the source of political movements which achieve change in a society.

- The Islamic revolution in Iran in 1979 was led by a fundamentalist Muslim religious leader. This movement was based on the revolutionary manifesto that pointed out how people had been deluded by a westernised ruling elite, and could be saved by returning to the true religion.
- The leader of the movement which gained independence for India in 1947, Mahatma Ghandi, used aspects of the Hindu belief (especially that which advocated freedom for all citizens) to encourage a rebellion against British rule.
- In both cases, the revolutionary leaders shared the same religion as the masses, which was different from the religion of those they were seeking to overthrow.
- All ethnic religious groups and organisations which have exclusive ethnic membership must impede the processes of assimilation, since they emphasise a solidarity based on language and culture.

WEBERIANS

Weber argued that religion can promote or impede social change:

1 Whereas most of the eastern religions emphasise mysticism, meditation and humility so that a good simple life may end in reincarnation in an improved form, Protestantism in the west promotes the work ethic. Weber showed how there was a relationship between the growth of Protestantism and the emergence of capitalism in the west.

2 He accepts that religion is a response to the misfortunes of life, providing explanations and offering ways of mediating with the supernatural world. Different groups (according to ethnicity and status) have different religious outlooks, because their experiences vary. Sect membership appeals to the disadvantaged.

Points of criticism

- Hamilton notes that perhaps it was not so much Protestantism which contributed to the development of rational capitalism, as the position of Calvinistic groups, who were marginal, underprivileged and therefore highly motivated to succeed.
- Hindus and Sikhs who came to Britain penniless in the early 1970s, have proved very effective and successful in business although their religion may be meditational.

PHENOMENOLOGISTS

Berger and Luckmann have argued that to understand social behaviour, it is necessary to understand the meanings which people act on, and how religion helps make sense of the world.

The need for structures to establish meaning

Ethnic minorities might make more use of religion than the host society because they in particular need plausibility structures to assist them to make sense of their new environment. It is religion which gives legitimation to the arbitrary and relative **universe of meaning**.

The power of culture

The majority of ethnic minorities make use of the religions with which they are familiar through their culture, because it is this which makes most sense to them. The values and beliefs of mainstream Christianity are unlikely to be attractive to someone whose social understanding has been shaped by a polytheistic religion or special dietary requirements which have no meaning in the new society.

Points of criticism

- Berger and Luckmann may overemphasise the significance of religion in providing plausibility structures, to give meaning and knowledge about the social and physical world.
- Not all members of ethnic minorities practise their religious traditions; they are able to find other mechanisms for coping with everyday problems of life, just as non-religious people do in any society.

Activity
List reasons why new immigrants retain a strong belief in traditional religious values. Under what conditions might they prefer to become involved in the dominant religion of the new society?

FUNDAMENTALISM: A CHALLENGE TO THE POSTMODERNIST VIEW

Gracie Davie notes how in the past, the examination of religion in advanced industrial societies frequently showed the churches and other religious organisations adapting to the processes of decline in religious observance. This helped to promote ideas relating to secularisation. However, she points out that such an approach is becoming harder to sustain, because it is full of contradictory interpretations. (See pp 87–89.)

The growing support for the ideas of **fundamentalism** have also presented new issues for the secularisation thesis. She argues that it is often incorrectly used when applied in a disparaging way about Christian sects or Islam, implying that they are the bizarre religions of fanatics. In fact, sociologists ought to use the term fundamentalism as a descriptive word that is concerned with certain kinds of religious movements in the contemporary, postmodern world. It describes those who wish to promote the basic truths of a well-established religion and enforce them with fervour to the conditions of twentieth century life. The emergence of fundamentalism on a large scale and across several continents in recent years has bewildered many commentators. It has questioned common sociological assumptions that the contemporary world is becoming more secular.

Study point
Suggest why the growth of fundamentalism raises problems for the secularisation thesis.

Fundamentalism was a term first used in the debates among American Protestants in the 1920s. There were attempts to re-establish traditional Protestant truths which had been threatened by liberal theological interpretations. Protestant fundamentals were established, which included an emphasis on the literal interpretation of the creation story, and a rejection of evolutionary theory. Subsequently, it has been applied to developments in

Islamic societies where traditional patterns of belief came under attack in a similar way. There is a clash between fundamentalist endeavours to recover the sacred part of social life and secure its values.

MODERNITY AND POSTMODERNISM

This concept arose in the late nineteenth century to distinguish 'modern' from 'premodern' or 'preindustrial' societies. *Modern* societies became synonymous with *industrial* societies, and understanding the changes that had occurred was the principal goal of sociology. In recent years, modern societies are contrasted with postmodern or postindustrial ones, and with new and different forms of industrial life. Modern society is no longer seen as the apex of human achievement. The link can be made between the growth of fundamentalism and the crises of modernity in years since the early 1970s. These included concerns about the loss of oil sources, pollution, ozone depletion, various economic problems, even the growth of feminism and debates about political correctness and equality.

The results of such debates in the secular, non-religious areas of social life, may have been to promote the spread of fundamentalism throughout the world. The belief was that unless traditional values were re-asserted, society would become destabilised. Religious fundamentalism is seen by Davie as a response to a combination of social and economic pressures. It is associated with:

- a rapid social change in the society
- internal and external threats to its stability or externally. Terms like westernisation, modernity or invasion are used
- a new powerful (usually religious) leader who emerges to focus discontented people
- a process of reaction – there is selective retrieval from the past
- the discovery of authority for the new actions (usually in a sacred text)
- new social boundaries which are established between the followers and the remainder.

Ironically, it seems to be the case that to achieve its ends, maximum use is made of new technology. Those seeking to resist modernity make optimum use of the system they regard as threatening their existence. Fundamentalisms are the products of modernity in the clash with tradition; a growth of uncertainty and insecurity in the lives of people.

There are consequences for the postmodern society, as new changes take hold.

- There may be a fragmenting of the traditional social structure so that the old class system is replaced by a new, more fluid one.
- There is a loss of confidence in the religious and secular stories that have been formulated over time to explain the difficulties of human existence.

- Intellectual thinking becomes freer as it escapes the controls of religious organisations. This is one of the features of secularisation.

Davie concludes that religious fundamentalism emerged to counteract the threats of modernism. More recently, in the postmodern world, the alternative ideologies have been prone to similar pressures, as secular and religious creeds have begun to fragment (eg, the collapse of Communist ideologies). In the quest for certainties to act as bulwarks against change, fundamentalist values emerge. They are, therefore, normal rather than abnormal features of postmodernity. They provide coping mechanisms in times of uncertainty.

Study point

Jehovah's Witnesses are described as a Christian fundamentalist sect. Why might their opposition to the ideas of evolution be an attempt for certainty?

SUMMARY

The religions of ethnic minorities are more successful in attracting membership than those of mainstream churches and denominations. This is due in part to the need of minorities to maintain a sense of identity and cultural defence within their communities. There is some evidence that as they adapt to the norms of the dominant society, they may become less religious.

STUDY GUIDES

Group work

Religious issues are widely covered in the press, radio and television.

- Monitor all forms of media for a week (including all daily and Sunday newspapers, as well as local press). Note the details of any television programmes, date all cuttings and include the source.
- Sort the cuttings and details recorded into categories (eg, information relating to sects, churches, ethnic minority religions, statistics). The chairperson should distribute them to group members.

- Each group should extract relevant information and present it to the whole group as a short conference paper. This should endeavour to illustrate the dominant themes of religion in the media in the course of the week selected.
- The appointed chairperson should conclude by drawing themes from the papers together.

Key Concepts Activity

Each group to define and discuss the terms listed on p 109, with examples from their own experience. Write the definition on a Key Concept Card for revision purposes (see p 3).

Practice questions

1 Account for the fact that ethnic minorities in Britain appear to be more religious in their attitudes and behaviour than the host society. Consider the implications for the secularisation thesis.
2 Examine the factors which may strengthen the sense of religious involvement in ethnic minorities and those which may serve to undermine it over time.
3 To what extent does their attachment to a religion help ethnic minorities to become established in British society?

Coursework suggestions

1 The strength of membership and practice of ethnic minority religions may vary between generations. Are there similar generational differences in local Christian churches?
2 How well informed are people about religious beliefs and practices of ethnic minorities? Are there differences in knowledge between church attenders and non church attenders? Are there differences between different age groups?

RELIGIOUS GROUPS IN BRITAIN

We would recommend that students do not become involved with any religious groups listed

Baha'i Faith
27 Rutland Gate
London SW7 1PD

Buddhism
58 Eccleston Square
London SW1V 1PH

Church of England
Church House
Great Smith Street
London SW1P 3NZ

Hinduism/Sikhism
4A Castletown Road
London W14 9HQ

Islam
Islamic Cultural Centre
Regent's Park Lodge
146 Park Road
London NW8 7RG

Judaism
Woburn House
Tavistock Square
London WC1H OEZ

Roman Catholicism
The Chase Centre
Catholic Enquiries
114 West Heath Road
London NW3 7TX

Sufism
Beauchamp Lodge
2 Warwick Crescent
London W2 6NE

Christadelphians
404 Shaftmoor Lane
Hall Green
Birmingham B28 8SZ

Christian Scientists
2 Elysium Gate
126 New King's Road
London SW6 4LZ

Evangelical Alliance
Whitefield House
186 Kennington Park Road
London SE11 4BT

Exclusive Bretheren
99 Green Lane
Hounslow
Middlesex TW4 6BW

Jehovah's Witnesses
IBSA House
The Ridgeway
London NW7 1RN

Jesus Army
Central Offices
Nether Heyford
Northampton NN7 3LB

Mormons
751 Warwick Road
Solihull
West Midland B91 3DQ

Opus Dei
6 Orme Court
London W2 4RL

Zoroastrianism
88 Compayne Gardens
London NW6 3RU

Seventh Day Adventists
Stanborough Park
Watford
Herts WD2 6JP

Unification Church (Moonies)
42-44 Lancaster Gate
London W2 3NA

Unitarians
1-6 Essex Street
Strand
London WC2R 3HY

Worldwide Church of God
PO Box 111
Boreham Wood
Herts WD6 1LU

ECKANKAR
PO Box 4496
London SW19 8XQ

Nichiren Shoshu
Taplow Court
Taplow
Maidenhead
Berks SL6 OER

Aetherius Society
757 Fulham Road
London SW6 5UU

Church Universal & Triumphant
Summit Lighthouse
65–66 Charlotte Road
London EC2A 3PE

Quakers
Friends House
Euston Road
London NW1 2BJ

Swedenborgians
Swedenborg House
20 Bloomsbury Way
London WC1A 2TH

United Church of God
PO Box 5929
Thatcham
Berks RG19 6YX

Elan Vital
PO Box 999
Hove
East Sussex BN3 1HX

ISKCON
Bhaktivedanta Manor
Letchmore Heath
Watford
Herts WD2 8EP

Osho International
24 St James's Street
London SW1A 1HA

Anthroposophy
Rudolph Steiner House
35 Park Road
London NW1 6XT

Emissaries
Mickleton House
Mickleton
Chipping Camden
Glos. GL55 6RY

Society of the Inner Light
38 Steele's Road
London NW3 4RG

Lectorium Rosicrucianum
BM LR7
London WC1N 3XX

Subud
Watton Villa
Brecon
Powys LD3 7HH

Servants of the Light
PO Box 215
St Helier
Jersey JE4 9SD
Channel Island

Theosophy
50 Gloucester Place
London W1H 4EA

Neo-Pagan Movements

**Eagle's Wing Centre for
Contemporary Shamanism**
58 Westbere Road
London NW2 3RU

Fellowship of Isis
Clonegal Castle
Enniscorthy
Eire

Findhorn Community
The Park
Findhorn
Forres IV36 OTZ
Scotland

Hoblink
Box 22
4-7 Dorset Street
Brighton
East Sussex BL2 1WA

House of the Goddess
33 Oldridge Road
London SW12 8PN

Isle of Avalon Foundation
The Courtyard
2–4 High Street
Glastonbury
Somerset BA6 9DU

Pagan Federation
BM Box 7097
London WC1N 3XX

British Druid Order
PO Box 29
St Leonards-on-sea
East Sussex TN37 7YP

Loyal Arthurian Warband
c/o 10 Sine Close
Farnborough
Hants GU14 8HG

Personal Development Movements

Emin
PO Box 48
Saffron Walden
Essex CB11 3PD

Insight
37 Spring Street
London W2 1JA

Scientology
Saint Hill Manor
East Grinsted
West Sussex RH19 4JY

Transcendental Meditation
Mentmore Towers
Mentmore
Leighton Buzzard
Beds LU7 OQH

Cult-Watching Organisations

Catalyst
The Bridge Centre
Spa Common
Retford
Notts DN22 6LQ

Cult Information Centre
BCM Cults
London WC1N 3XX

Inform
Houghton Street
London WC2A 2AE

Deo Gloria Outreach
Selsdon House
212–220 Addington Road
South Croydon
Surrey CR2 8LD

Reachout Trust
24 Ormond Road
Richmond
Surrey TW10 6TH

Cult Awareness Network
2421 West Pratt Blvd
Suite 1173
Chicago
IL 60645
USA

FURTHER READING

THE NATURE AND MEANING OF RELIGION

In light of ecological concerns and the attempts to conserve land designated for road building in the 1990s, students may be interested to read Chapter 9 'The Worship of Trees' in *The Golden Bough: A Study in Magic and Religion*; Frazer, J.G. (Macmillan 1995).

For information about particular faiths, what they believe, their traditions and where they are found, see Bishop, P. & Darton, M. (eds) (1987) *The Encyclopedia of World Faiths: An Illustrated Survey of the World's Living Religions*, Macdonald Orbis. Also Hinnels, J. (ed) (1988) *A Handbook of Living Religions*, Penguin.

Marshall, G. 'The Protestant Ethic', *Sociology Review* Vol 1 No 1 1991.

Hadden, J. (1987) 'Towards Desacrilizing Secularisation Theory', *Social Forces*, 65, 3 (an abridged version of this article is in Giddens, A. (ed) (1997) *Sociology: Introductory Readings*, Polity Press).

Smart, N. (1989) *The World's Religions*, Cambridge University Press

Beit-Hallahmi, B. (1993) *The Illustrated Encyclopedia of Active New Religions, Sects and Cults*, Rosen

SOCIOLOGY DICTIONARIES AND REFERENCE BOOKS

For helpful definitions of terms and concepts the reader is recommended to use Lawson, T., and Garrod, J. (1996) *The Complete A-Z Sociology Handbook*, Hodder and Stoughton.

Kuper, A. & Kuper, J. (1996) *The Social Science Encyclopedia*, Routledge.

Jary, D. & Jary, J. (1995) *Collins Dictionary of Sociology* (second edition), Harper Collins

Melton, G., Clark, J, & Kelly, A. (1991) *New Age Almanac*, New York: Visible Ink.

UK Christian Handbook (1998/99), Carlisle: Paternoster Publications

MAGIC, SUPERSTITION AND SCIENCE

Cavendish, R. (1980) *History of Magic*, Taplinger

Neusner, J., Frerichs, E. & Flesher, P. (eds) *Religion, Science and Magic*, OUP

Wilson, B. (1975) *Magic and the Millennium*, Paladin. He provides many interesting examples of millennial movements; those in Chapter 10, concerned with cargo cults, is a readable example.

SOCIOLOGY OF RELIGION

Bruce, S. (1996) *Religion in the Modern World: From Cathedrals to Cults*, OUP

Hamilton, M. (1995) *The Sociology of Religion: Theoretical and Comparative Perspectives*, Routledge. (Chapters 6, 8 & 12 may be especially useful.)

Davie, G. *Religion in Britain Since 1945* (1996) Blackwell. See Chapter 5 in which she discusses 'believing without belonging'.

Hastings, A. (1986) *A History of English Christianity 1929–1985*. Collins

RELIGIOUS MEMBERSHIP AND ATTENDANCE IN BRITAIN

Social Trends No 27 (1997). Published each year in November, it provides valuable statistical data.

Jowell, R., Brook, L., Prior, G & Taylor B. (eds) (1992) *British Social Attitudes: 9th Report*, Aldershot and Dartmouth.

RELIGIONS OF ETHNIC MINORITY GROUPS

Pryce, K. (1979) *Endless Pressure. A Study of West Indian Lifestyles*, Penguin

Kalsi, S. (1992) *The Evolution of a Sikh Community in Britain*, University of Leeds

Nielsen, J. (1992) *Muslims in Western Europe*, Edinburgh University Press

Butler, C. 'Religion and Gender', *Sociology Review*, Vol 4, No 3, 1995

Wilson, B. & Dobbelaere, K. (1994) *A Time to Chant*

NEW RELIGIOUS MOVEMENTS

Barker, E. (1989) *New Religious Movements; A Practical Introduction*, HMSO

Heelas, P., *The New Age; Celebrating the Self*, Blackwell.

Wallis, R. 'The Sociology of the New Religions' *Social Studies Review*, Vol 1, No 1, 1985

Hallsworth, S. 'Understanding New Social Movements' *Sociology Review*, Vol 4, No 1, 1994

Luhrman, T. (1989) *Persuasions of the Witch's Craft*, Blackwell.

Beckford, J. (1985) *Cult Controversies*, Tavistock.

ENTERTAINING AND CONTROVERSIAL

Baigent, M., Leigh, R., & Lincoln, H. (1987) *The Messianic Legacy* Corgi. ('Was there more than one Christ? What do the Nuremberg Rallies and rock concerts have in common?)

Bedoyere, M. (1964) *Objections to Roman Catholicism*, Constable

Mystics and Prophets, Ritual and Magic, UFOs, (1997) Orbis Publishing
See also those listed on p 97.
Osborn, L. and Walker, A. (1997) *Harmful Religions,* London: SPCK

JOURNALS

- Journal for the Scientific Study of Religion
- Religion
- Social Compass
- Sociology of Religion
- Sociology Review

RESOURCES AND WEB SITES

Other resources to investigate in which there may be useful information or advice:

- The web site of the **Association for the Teaching of Social Sciences** which may provide information about possible source material. The URL is <http://www.le.ac.uk/education/centres/ATSS/atss.html>
- The Microsoft Encarta Encyclopedia.
- Network: The Newsletter of the British Sociological Association (Email: britsoc@dial.pipex).
  WWW Virtual Library: Sociology – http://www.fisk.edu/vl/Sociology/Overview.html
  The Socioweb – http://www.socioweb.com/-markbl/socioweb/
  Sociosite – http://www.pscw.uva.nl/sociosite/index.html
  WWW Virtual Library: Religion – http://sunfly.ub.uni-freiburg.de/religion/
  Comparative Religion – http://weber.u.washington.edu/-madin/

VIDEOS

See the British Universities Film and Video Council's entire database on CD-ROM for details of audio visual materials for secondary and higher education. It contains details of 18,000 titles available on film, videotape and other media including computer based multimedia.

The Religious Studies Department at your school or college may have the following videos:
Judasim: Religion of a People; Hinduism: An Ancient Path in the Modern World; Buddhism: The Middle Way of Compassion; Islam – The Faith and the People: A World-Wide Influence; Half a Kingdom (Jewish women); Black Pentecostal Experience; Educational Media Film and Video Ltd.

INDEX